Peoples and Nations of the
AMERICAS

*A short history of each country
in North, Central, and South America,
and the Caribbean Sea*

Sheila Fairfield

Gareth Stevens Publishing
Milwaukee

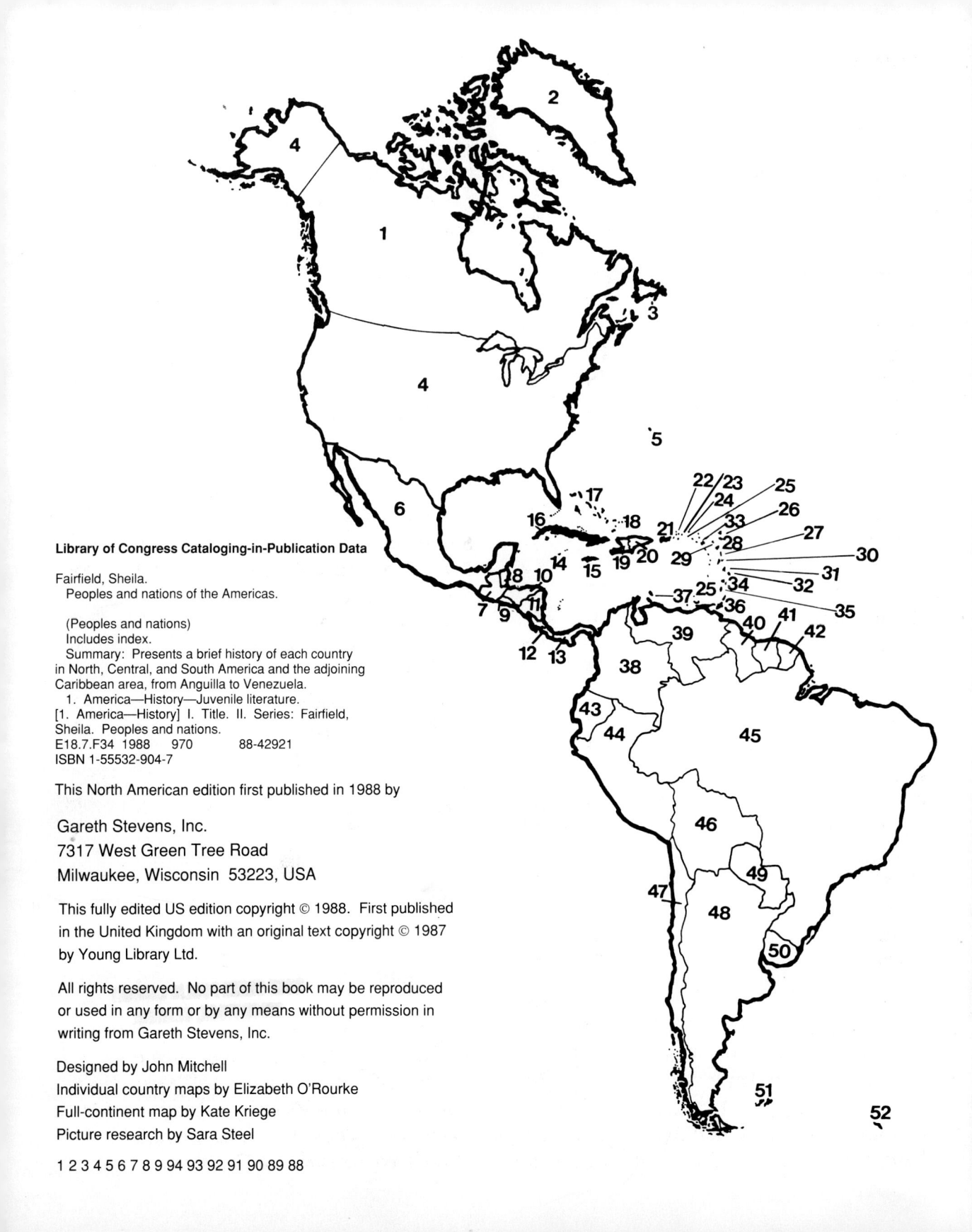

Library of Congress Cataloging-in-Publication Data

Fairfield, Sheila.
 Peoples and nations of the Americas.

 (Peoples and nations)
 Includes index.
 Summary: Presents a brief history of each country in North, Central, and South America and the adjoining Caribbean area, from Anguilla to Venezuela.
 1. America—History—Juvenile literature.
[1. America—History] I. Title. II. Series: Fairfield, Sheila. Peoples and nations.
E18.7.F34 1988   970   88-42921
ISBN 1-55532-904-7

This North American edition first published in 1988 by

Gareth Stevens, Inc.
7317 West Green Tree Road
Milwaukee, Wisconsin 53223, USA

This fully edited US edition copyright © 1988. First published in the United Kingdom with an original text copyright © 1987 by Young Library Ltd.

All rights reserved. No part of this book may be reproduced or used in any form or by any means without permission in writing from Gareth Stevens, Inc.

Designed by John Mitchell
Individual country maps by Elizabeth O'Rourke
Full-continent map by Kate Kriege
Picture research by Sara Steel

1 2 3 4 5 6 7 8 9 94 93 92 91 90 89 88

CONTENTS

	Map	Text		Map	Text
Anguilla	24	30	**Mexico**	6	14
Antigua and Barbuda	26	36	**Montserrat**	29	36
Argentina	48	55	**Netherlands Antilles**	25	30
Aruba	37	41	**Nicaragua**	11	22
The Bahamas	17	29	**Panama**	13	25
Barbados	32	37	**Paraguay**	49	52
Belize	8	19	**Peru**	44	59
Bermuda	5	13	**Puerto Rico**	21	37
Bolivia	46	41	**St. Kitts-Nevis**	33	38
Brazil	45	48	**St. Lucia**	31	35
British Virgin Islands	22	32	**St. Pierre and Miquelon**	3	7
Canada	1	4	**St. Vincent and**		
Cayman Islands	14	28	**the Grenadines**	34	29
Chile	47	57	**South Georgia and the South**		
Colombia	38	44	**Sandwich Islands**	52	57
Costa Rica	12	24	**Suriname**	41	47
Cuba	16	27	**Trinidad and Tobago**	36	39
Dominica	27	38	**The Turks and**		
Dominican Republic	20	34	**Caicos Islands**	18	30
Ecuador	43	53	**United States of America**	4	8
El Salvador	9	20	**United States**		
The Falkland Islands	51	57	**Virgin Islands**	23	32
French Guiana	42	46	**Uruguay**	50	43
Greenland	2	14	**Venezuela**	39	39
Grenada	35	34	**Glossary**		62
Guadeloupe	28	38	**Index**		63
Guatemala	7	17			
Guyana	40	51			
Haiti	19	32			
Honduras	10	21			
Jamaica	15	23			
Martinique	30	31			

A note on the entries in this book: Each nation-state and dependency has a written entry and its own map or a reference to a map elsewhere in the book. Also, some countries include lands that are geographically separated from the main area. These lands do not have a separate entry but are included in the main country's entry. Finally, some countries are mentioned that are part of other continents. They do not have entries here, but you can find them in other volumes of the *Peoples and Nations* series.

The Mounties, pictured above as they are today, were formed in 1873 to bring law and order to the Canadian wilderness.

CANADA

Canada is a vast North American country, north of the United States. South of the Arctic Circle the mainland is nearly divided by the Rocky Mountains in the west and Hudson Bay in the east. Within the circle, north of the mainland, lies a scattering of Canadian islands.

The early people of the Americas probably came from northeast Asia across a strip of land that used to bridge the Bering Strait. The people on the west coast lived on river salmon, sea fish, and forest game. Food was easy to find, and people had time and energy to become skilled artisans.

In the ice of the far north the Inuits, or Eskimos, and Aleuts hunted for fish, seals, and caribou. In the vast wilderness south of the ice lived many small groups of hunters. Their life was hard, and they fought each other for what little food there was. In the long winters many starved. When they began a trade in animal furs, they fought over that as well.

The people of the woods in southeast Canada also had a fur trade. They lived in large villages and grew much of their food where they had made clearings in the trees. They were the first to meet settlers from Europe in the early seventeenth century. The early explorers called all native North American people "Indians" because they thought they had discovered India.

The English and Scots built small settlements near the east coast, but Frenchmen moved further inland with the fur trade. In 1608 they founded Quebec as a trading post and from there traveled far inland. They explored the country and came to know the

Indians who sold them animal skins. They married Indian women and their children were called *métis*, which means "mixed."

To protect their business and defend their suppliers from enemies, the French joined in the Indian wars. They sided with the Algonquin and Huron Indians against the Iroquois. The wars went on for years.

In 1670 the British entered the fur trade and set up the Hudson's Bay Company. Rivalry between the British and the French often became violent, because they were on opposite sides in wars being fought in Europe. Their war in Canada ended in 1763, with all the French land in Canada being granted to Britain.

The British now had to learn to govern a place with few British settlers, many French towns and villages, and a large number of Indian nations. After many mistakes they worked out a type of government that seemed to suit the Catholic French in Quebec colony.

But then came the War of Independence in Britain's American colonies further south. Then colonists won, and British refugees,

The spectacular Rocky Mountains stride down the west side of North America from Alaska to Mexico.

A woman from the village of Pierre St. Jaques spins wool as her ancestors did hundreds of years ago.

called loyalists, fled to Canada from the colonies. But the system of government that suited the French did not suit the British, and in 1791 the government divided Quebec colony into Upper Canada, mainly British, and Lower Canada, mainly French. The refugees also founded New Brunswick next to the Scots settlers in Nova Scotia, "New Scotland." In the southeast, Indian lands were set aside and protected.

The colonies lay along the St. Lawrence River and the shores of the Great Lakes. In 1867 they came together as the Dominion of Canada. Then they began to organize the wild country to the west and north, where many more Indians, métis, and the trappers and traders of the Hudson's Bay Company lived. But the fur trade became less important as the country began to make more money by using the land. The people grew wheat on the prairies. Even desolate places provided timber, metal ores, and crude oil. Fast-flowing rivers made cheap electricity

Quebec was founded by the French in 1608. Here is a sketch picturing how it looked in 1759, the year it fell to the British.

The picture below shows one of Henry Hudson's voyages of exploration to the Americas.

that many industries were eager to use.

The fur trade depended on the Indians, but the new farms and industries did not need them at all. Some Indians learned to work in mines or fish canneries, but sometimes they were left with no hunting grounds and no way to make a living.

Canada is now independent. English and French are both official languages. Roman Catholicism is the dominant religion. French Canadians have discussed whether to set up a nation of their own in Quebec, but so far, they have voted against doing this.

ST. PIERRE AND MIQUELON

St. Pierre and Miquelon is an overseas part of France. The territory comprises eight small islands off the southern coast of Newfoundland, in eastern Canada. These islands were colonized by French settlers in the seventeenth century. The people are mostly French-speaking Roman Catholics of French descent. Fishing is the main activity. (See map on page 6.)

7

Natchez, a tribe with customs like those of people in Mexico. Their ruler was the high priest of a sun god to whom they built temples. The Creeks settled on river banks, the Choctaws and Chickasaws in the inland woods. They all farmed, hunted, and trained young warriors. The Cherokees lived on either side of the Appalachian

The traditional dwelling of American Indians is the tepee, made from animal skins stretched on wooden poles.

The colorful dancer below is a member of the Hidatsa tribe, who lived by the Missouri river.

General Sherman's Union forces, right, march through Georgia during the US Civil War.

UNITED STATES OF AMERICA

The United States stretches from the Pacific to the Atlantic oceans. There are semitropical swamplands near the Gulf of Mexico and severe, snowy winters in the north. The east end of its border with Canada runs through the Great Lakes. Part of its Mexican border runs through hot desert. The United States also includes Alaska, which extends into the Arctic Circle northwest of Canada. (See map on page 6.) The other state not attached to the mainland is Hawaii.

The first mainland Americans came from Asia across the Bering Strait. They were the Aleuts, Inuits, and the people who are now called American Indians.

The Aleuts and Inuits settled in Alaska and the Aleutian Islands to hunt and fish. Others kept moving south. By AD 1500 there were many different peoples and cultures all over North America.

In the southeastern forests lived the

Mountains. Further north was a group with a similar language, the great union of Iroquois tribes. These speakers of Algonquian included the Blackfoot, Cheyenne, and Mohican tribes.

Forests ran westward to the vast river basin where the Mississippi, Missouri, and Ohio rivers join. Beyond the basin lay the Great Plains, grazed by millions of buffalo. Along the eastern edge of the plains lived the Sioux, Dakota, Pawnee, Iowa, Kansas, and other Indian tribes.

Nomadic Indians who lived on the plains and beyond in the Rocky Mountains included hunters and warriors such as the Blackfoot, Comanche, Kiowa, and Apache. But further southwest lived people who were quite different. They were the Pueblo Indians, skilled farmers who did not live in the usual villages. They built great stone terraces full of cell-like rooms. Their neighbors, and sometimes enemies, were the southern Apache and Navajo.

West coast people were mainly farmers, except in the northwest. There the heavily wooded coast had so much wild food that life was quite luxurious.

Europeans began settling the east coast as early as 1565, but came in greater numbers in the seventeenth century. Many came to Massachusetts. English merchants set up cash-crop and trading colonies in Virginia. Dutch traders in what is now New York dealt with Indian trappers for beaver and buckskin. Sometimes Indians and settlers profited from each other. Sometimes they went to war — usually over land.

At about the same time, Spanish-ruled

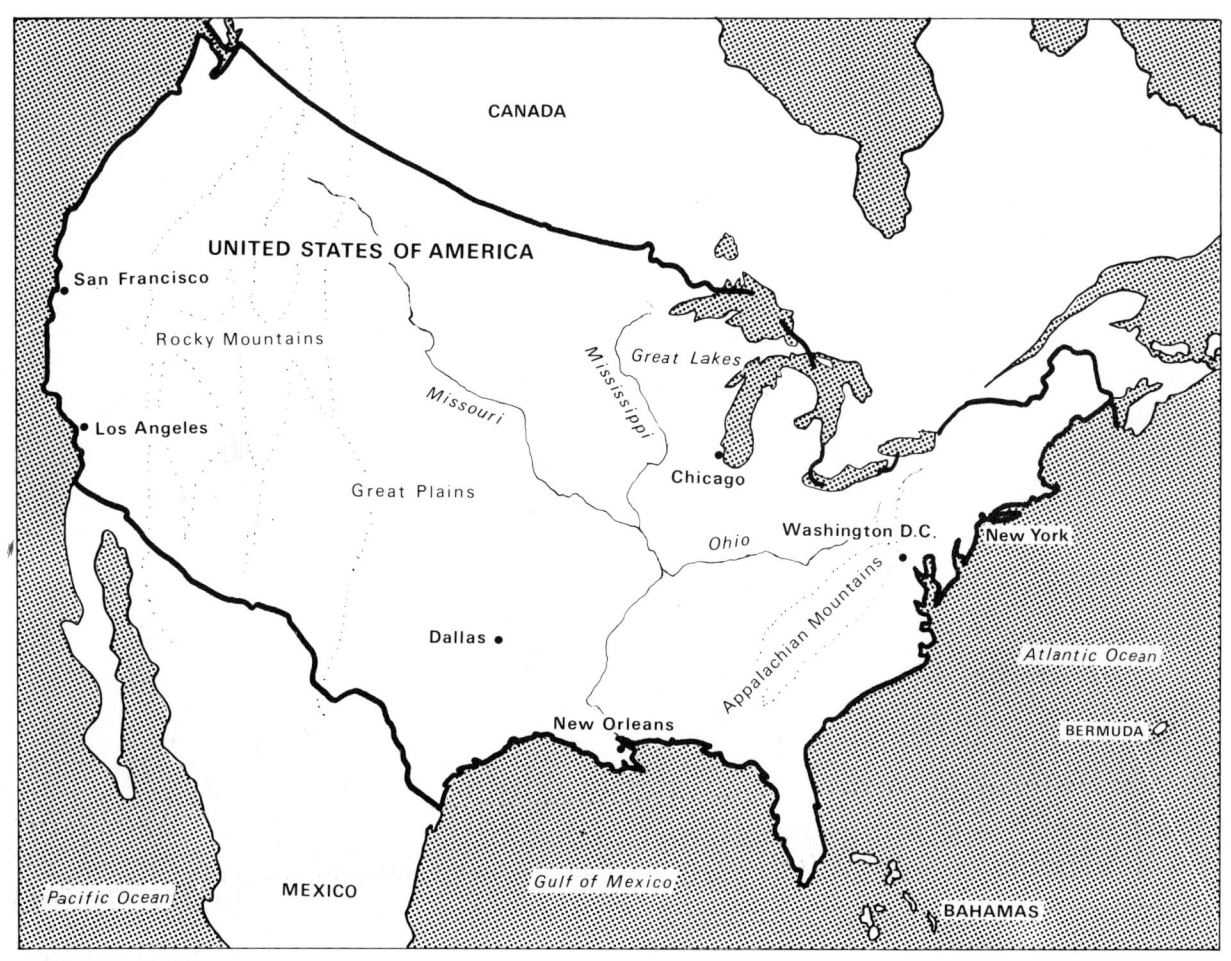

Mexico expanded north. Spain already held Florida, and now Spanish Catholic missionaries came into what is now Texas, New Mexico, Arizona, and southern California. Spanish-Mexican ranchers came too. From them the southern Apache and Kiowa discovered the horse. Gradually the art of horseback riding spread, so Comanche, Cheyenne, Arapaho, Crow, and others left the Rocky Mountains and the woodland villages to live as mounted buffalo hunters on the plains.

In the east in 1673, the Dutch came under English rule, and the coast became a string of English colonies from New England to South Carolina. New England was cold; the land was poor, and farming was hard work. The people worked in lumbering, fishing, shipbuilding, small manufacturing, and trade. They lived together in small towns under the strict Puritan religious laws. There were African slaves in New England, but fewer than in the south, and their work was more varied. The south had big plantations, with houses far apart and surrounded by rich land. Cash crops were grown by large groups of slaves owned by white settlers. Not all white settlers owned such plantations, but those who did were powerful.

The slaves were obtained mainly from the West African coast, between Accra and the Congo mouth, or from regions just inland. Others came from the edge of the Sahara desert or the Congo forests. There was a long tradition of slave trading by Arabs, and various tribes would also sell their prisoners of war. In South Carolina there was even a trade in Indian slaves.

Surviving coastal Indians fell back beyond the Appalachians to join the powerful Iroquois, Cherokees, and Creeks. Further west were more Europeans — the French, trading along the Mississippi from a flourishing base at New Orleans. Anglo-French

The picture above shows John Cabot and his sons landing in North America. They first sighted Nova Scotia in 1497.

General Ulysses Grant led the armies of the Union to victory over the Confederates in the US Civil War. The picture below shows him, seated third from left, holding a meeting with his staff.

wars included Indian allies on both sides. In 1763 the French withdrew. Without French support, the Indians could not stop the eastern settlers from spreading west.

By that time about half the settlers were from Continental Europe. Among them were the Huguenots, Protestant refugees. Protestant Germans and German-speaking Swiss joined English Quakers in Pennsylvania, where they were wrongly labeled Pennsylvania Dutch because the German word for "German" is *Deutsch*. Other Protestant immigrants, such as Northern Irish, Swedes,

The picture on the left shows an Indian village, defended by a wall of stakes.

Many US states have state celebrations. Below, Chicago turns out in style for Illinois Day.

The picture on the right shows the Pioneer Woman statue which stands in Ponca City, Oklahoma. It was erected in honor of early settlers.

Danes, and Norwegians, included prosperous citizens, merchants, farmers, and craftsmen, as well as beggars, tramps, and thieves.

In 1783 came freedom from British rule, and the foundation of the United States. The north abolished slavery, but the south kept it. New settlers like the Irish came to escape British rule in Ireland. Others, like the Germans and French, escaped the horrors of war and revolution.

During the nineteenth century, settlement spread westward across the continent. The southwest was won from Mexico, but Spanish language and customs remained. Spanish-Mexican cattle ranching on open ranges with mounted cowboys spread north from Texas. Cattle took over the plains as the great buffalo herds were destroyed by hunters and ranches grew larger.

In the east, slavery, regional differences, and the goal of preventing the southern states from seceding from the Union led to the US Civil War (1861-65). The South lost, and an important result was that it had to abandon slavery.

By the 1880s the United States was known as a country where people could find a better way of life. Thousands came to try. Some succeeded, and some failed. The Chinese and Japanese came to the west coast; the poor from all over Europe poured into the east. They did not come to settle land this time, but to find work.

Today there are still areas, especially in large cities, that have strong Polish, Italian, Chinese, or other immigrant communities. More than half of all black US citizens still live in the southeast. English is the official language. The majority of religious believers follow Christian faiths.

BERMUDA

Bermuda, a British colony, is a group of very small islands about 570 miles (917 km) east of North Carolina in the Atlantic Ocean. British settlers began arriving in 1612. They brought African slaves with them and bought more once they arrived.

Twenty islands are inhabited. Most people are of African ancestry; the rest are British or Portuguese. The people practice various forms of Christianity, and the major language is English, although some Portuguese is spoken as well.

Because of its mild climate, Bermuda is a famous winter resort. The capital is Hamilton, and the other major town is St. George. (See map on page 10.)

The Vikings sailed west 500 years before Columbus landed in the West Indies. Here, Eric the Red arrives in Greenland in AD 983.

GREENLAND

An enormous island, Greenland lies northeast of Canada. Most of it is within the Arctic Circle. Greenland is an overseas part of Denmark. It became a Danish colony in 1721, but Norwegians, led by Eric the Red, had been settling for centuries before that.

The people work mainly in the fishing industry. About one-sixth of the people are immigrant Danes, but most are Inuits, or Eskimos, and their language is called Greenlandic. Danish is spoken as well, and the Lutheran Church of Denmark is the official religion. (See map on page 6.)

MEXICO

Mexico is a large country that lies between the United States and Central America. Much of it is within the tropics, but it is mountainous and can be cool. The Gulf of Campeche coast, however, is low-lying and hot. There the Olmecs lived, worshipping the gods of rain and fertility. They built their cities around great temples and chased the jaguar as their sacred beast.

After 200 BC the people of central Mexico became more active. The two ranges of the Sierra Madre mountains meet at their southern end, enclosing a high plateau. South of their meeting is a sheltered valley of lakes and woods. The city of Teotihuacán was about 33 miles (50 km) northeast of modern Mexico City. It had all the ideas that survived from the Olmec cities and others that lasted through Mexican civilization until the Spanish conquest of 1521.

Teotihuacán had a vast religious area,

laid out on a grid pattern. The people built temples on platforms or pyramids. They worshipped the great god Quetzalcóatl, which means "the Feathered Serpent." The priesthood held great power, and strict rules governed the people's lives. A city of great art and architecture, most of it in stone, Teotihuacán lasted until about AD 900, when the Toltecs destroyed the city. Similar centers outlived it, like those of the Zapotek and Mixtec people in Oaxaca. But some things changed. Priests demanded more human sacrifice. A warrior class became powerful, capturing in war those who were to be sacrificed in the temple.

An escort of soldiers guards a shipment of silver on its way from the mines to Mexico City.

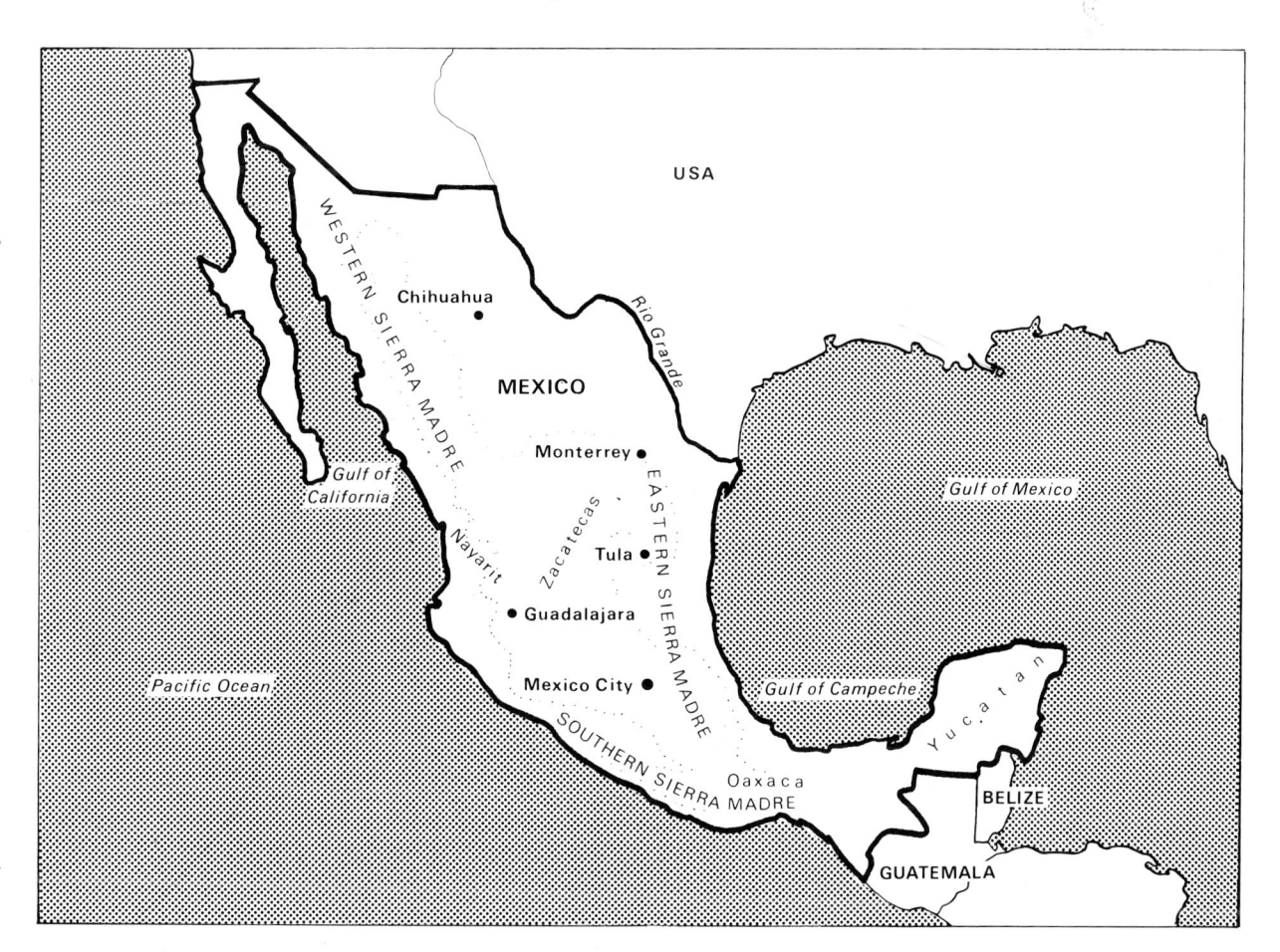

Two young Mexican girls, left, deliver lunch to workers in the fields.

Opposite are the ruins of Chichén Itzá, an ancient Mayan city in southeast Mexico.

Once Teotihuacán had fallen, groups of rough, nomadic nations moved down from the north into the valley. The Toltecs of Zacatecas came about AD 900. They founded Tula, and from there their power spread south. Toltecs were energetic and intelligent warriors. They adopted many of the ways of people living in the valleys.

In southeastern Mexico the Mayan people were the strongest. From Guatemala they had moved into Yucatán. Their best time (AD 300-600) was over when the Toltecs reached them, but their work in writing with picture symbols, astronomy, and the calendar was very significant.

Although they practiced human sacrifice, the Maya were fairly peaceful. The next northern invaders were not. The Aztecs came down from Nayarit after 1200. They called themselves Nahua and their language Nahuatl. They worshipped a god requiring frequent human sacrifices. The Aztecs conquered much of Mexico from their lake-island city, Tenochtitlán. In 1521 they themselves were conquered by Spain. The Spaniards destroyed Tenochtitlán and drained the lake. They then built Mexico City in its place.

Spain had invaded the Americas to convert them to the Roman Catholic faith and to win treasure and glory for the Spanish king. Missionaries began work in Mexico, as did men looking for gold and silver. The Spaniards brought in cattle, horses, and sheep. They turned north Mexico into ranching country, living as they were used to in the highlands of Spain. Silver was found in the north. Tropical cash crops were planted on the long, hot coast of the Gulf of Mexico.

The Aztec and earlier rulers had slaves and forced labor. The Spaniards carried on both traditions. When there were not enough Mexican workers, they imported West African slaves. Most Mexican profits went to Spain. As time passed, many people — whether Spanish, Mexican, or of mixed descent — wanted independence. It came in 1821, but only after war. Years of upheaval followed.

Mexico lost its northern regions to the United States. Foreign countries interfered with the government. People of Spanish birth and descent, those of mixed descent, and original Mexicans — all battled for advantage over one another.

By 1910 there was much modern industry and foreign investment. But the profits went to a few, not to the thousands of poor peasants. For ten years there was civil war — the Mexican Revolution — leading to a new republic.

Much that is modern in Mexico has been influenced by the United States, but Mexico has a distinct, unique culture, and the official language is still Spanish. People also speak Nahuatl, Zapotec, Mixtec, Maya, and at least fifty other languages. The main religion is Roman Catholicism.

GUATEMALA

Guatemala is a country in Central America near Mexico, Belize, El Salvador, and Honduras. It has great marshland and forests in the north, and its center is mountainous.

The Mayan people lived in northern Guatemala perhaps as early as 2500 BC. Tikal became their greatest city. They built pyramid temples there for the gods of the sun, moon, and rain. The Maya became powerful through their religion and through their mastery of writing and calculating. They were not very warlike, so they were easily overrun by the Toltecs and Aztecs of Mexico after 900.

The Mexican conquerors were themselves conquered by Spain, who ruled Guatemala from 1524 until 1821. They used

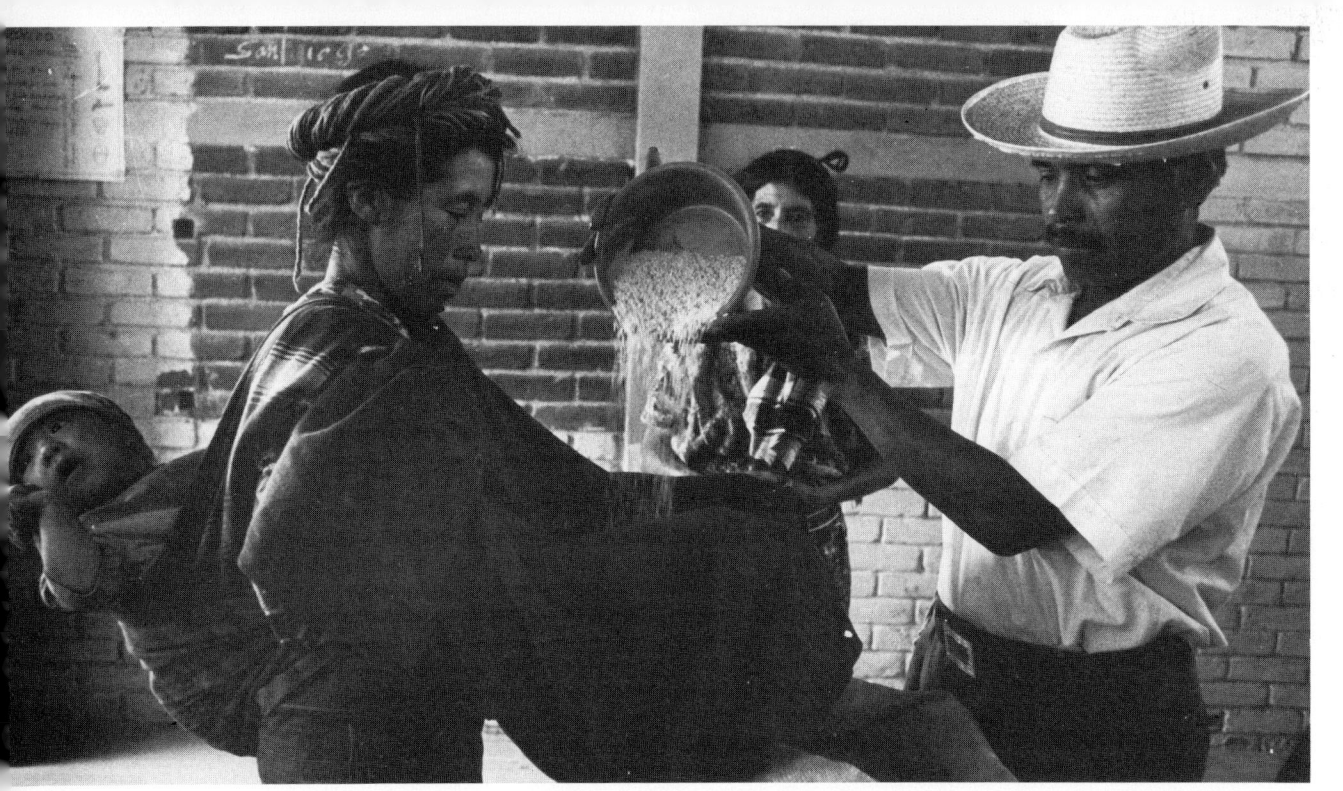

Mayan and African slave labor to work cash-crop plantations. But Guatemala never became a strong part of the Spanish empire. Earthquakes and volcanoes destroyed the cities, and pirates raided the coast. The great Mayan centers in the north became deserted, and most people lived in the southern hills.

From 1823 to 1829 Guatemala was part of a Central American union of neighboring countries. Future leaders tried to revive this union but failed. Guatemala has remained a single, independent republic since 1839. Its history has been violent.

More than half the people are of Mayan ancestry. The rest are mainly of mixed Mayan-Spanish stock. The official language is Spanish, although Maya and related languages are also used. Spanish Roman Catholicism is the main religion.

Central and South America suffer from earthquakes. Here a homeless Guatemalan woman and her child receive a ration of rice.

BELIZE

Belize is a small country on the east coast of Central America. Its northern coastal land is swampy and flat; inland and to the south are forests and mountains.

The mountains are called the Maya Mountains. The Mayan people, who have lived there for centuries, came from Guatemala and spread into Belize and Mexico. The early Maya produced clever systems of picture writing and had a sophisticated calendar. They lost their power by AD 900, but their descendants can still be found in the hill country.

From about 1638 British woodcutters came to the coast from Jamaica. Using African slaves, they cut into the great tropical forests, living in camps while they took valuable timber to sell. In theory the coast belonged to Spain, but no one lived there, and in time Spain handed control to Britain.

The logging camps developed into an industry, with slave labor and a growing port. Some slaves were African and some, called "Black Caribs," were descendants of African and Carib ancestors.

In 1847-53 a war in neighboring Mexico forced many Mexican refugees into northern Belize. In 1859 the boundary with Guatemala was established, but Guatemala has never accepted it completely.

The territory became the colony of British Honduras in 1862 and independent Belize in 1981. English is the official language, but people also speak Spanish, Maya, and Creole, a mixture of English and other languages. About half the population is Roman Catholic, and the remainder Anglican, Methodist, and Baha'i.

Belize women grating cassava, a tropical root vegetable, to make bread.

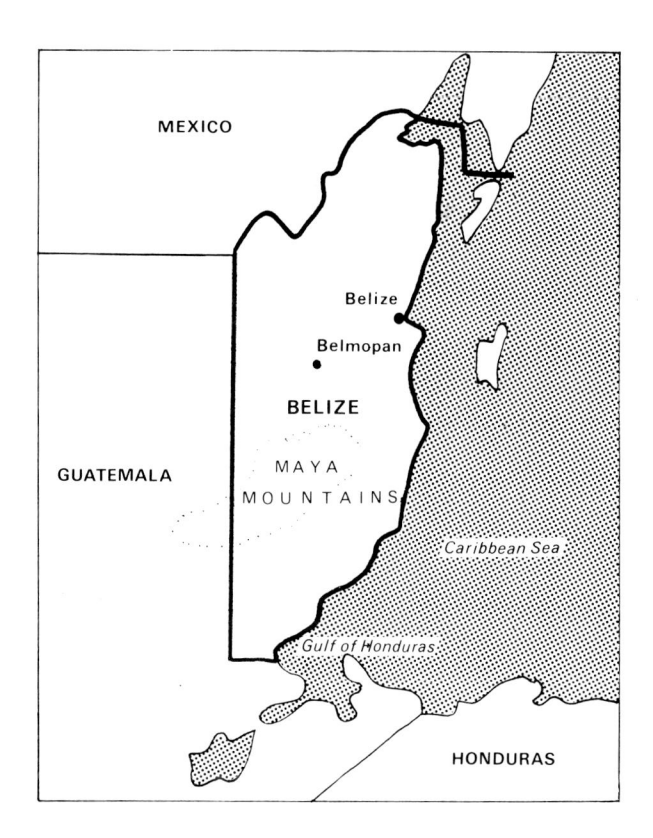

This square in Santa Ana, El Salvador, shows clearly the Spanish influence on the development of the cities and on their architecture.

EL SALVADOR

El Salvador is the smallest country of Central America and the most crowded. It lies on the Pacific Coast between Honduras and Guatemala. Most of the people live on a high, fertile volcanic plateau.

The early people, who farmed small areas and fished, were conquered by the Aztecs of Mexico. The Aztec empire fell to the Spaniards, who conquered El Salvador around 1526. It remained a farming country and became quite prosperous. The Spaniards founded San Miguel and San Vicente as new cities, and the original people met to trade at their center, Cihuatehuacán, now Santa Ana. Many of them adopted Spanish customs, language, and religion.

Spanish rule ended by 1821. By then most people were of mixed Spanish-Indian ancestry, Spanish-speaking, and Roman Catholic. There were African slaves on coastal plantations. The country was united with its neighbors from 1823-41 and became the independent republic of El Salvador in 1859.

From about 1880 the coffee industry supported the country. Foreign companies invested in the industry, and land was held by a few rich men who also planted cotton, which was quite successful. The government protected industry from uprisings by unhappy workers, but in 1944 the people revolted against their dictatorship.

El Salvador was crowded and most people were poor. Families began to move illegally across the frontier into Honduras. But Honduras was not rich enough to provide for thousands of poor peasants from El Salvador. They were sent back in crowds, and the problem led to war between El Salvador and Honduras in 1969.

By the time the war with Honduras had been settled there was civil war in El Salvador itself. El Salvador remains a divided and troubled nation to this day.

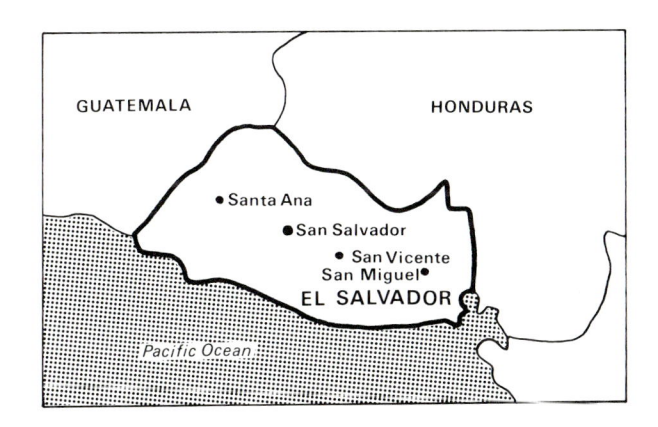

Coffee is a valuable export crop grown in many Central and South American countries.

HONDURAS

Honduras is a republic in Central America. It has a very short coastline on the Pacific side and a long Caribbean shore. The Caribbean side has thick forests, hot, sticky jungle, and a fertile lowland.

Today most people live in the central hills, which were also the most important area for the original people, the Maya and their related tribes. Copan in the west was a city of Mayan temples. From there, villages of farming, fishing, and hunting people spread eastward into the jungles.

Between 1502 and 1550 the Spaniards conquered Honduras. They settled in the south in 1524, found silver in the mountains, and built a town at Tegucigalpa, which is now the capital. Although the Spaniards did very little with the northern coast, pirates used it for their bases. British timber merchants came to the great tropical forests for mahogany, while in the mountains Spanish silver miners and other settlers used local labor and married local women. In time, most Hondurans were used to the Spanish way of life, could speak Spanish, and had some Spanish blood.

On the coasts the Spaniards had cash-crop plantations and used slave labor. The slaves came from Africa by way of the West Indies. The same mingling took place between local tribes, like the Miskito, and the Africans. Descendants of this mixed ancestry are called Zambos. Pure Miskitos, with their own language, still live in the east.

The country became independent of Spain in 1821. For a time Honduras was part of a Central American Union with Guatemala and other neighboring countries, but

A sketch of the settlement at Tiger Island, Honduras, in 1850. It is now the country's major port on the Pacific.

in 1838 it became an independent republic. Honduras was poor, and the mountains kept people apart and made travel and trade difficult.

After 1900 foreign investments brought change. Fruit companies from the United States built plantations on the coast. San Pedro Sula became the center of this new activity, and many people moved to the northern coast from the mountains.

Modern Honduras has a mixed population in the plantation areas. Elsewhere most people are descended from Mayan, Miskito, and other native groups, with some Spanish blood. Spanish is the official language and Roman Catholicism the main religion.

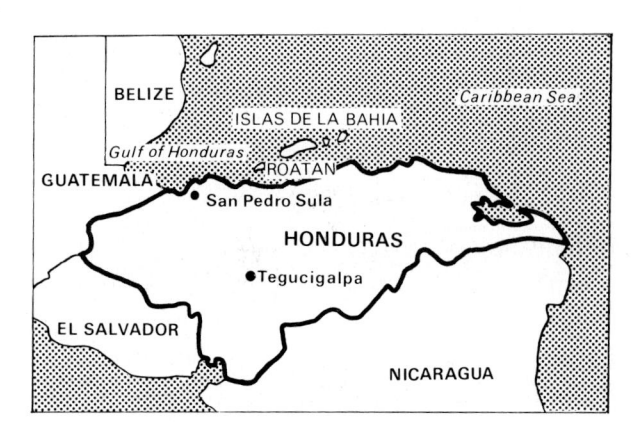

NICARAGUA

Nicaragua is a republic in Central America between Costa Rica and Honduras. In the west is lowland, with the big lakes of Managua and Nicaragua. This lowland is where most people live. The area has a rich soil that comes from the ash of more than twenty volcanoes. Some are still active. Central Nicaragua is mountainous. The east is low-lying jungle, swampy and hot. The eastern coast is called the Mosquito Coast.

Original people included the Miskito of the eastern jungles, mountain tribes, and the Nicarao, who lived on the west coast and had the best land. They were rich — so rich that they attracted stronger people looking for riches, and the Aztecs of Mexico had some control over them before their own conquest by the Spaniards in 1521.

The Spaniards came to Nicaragua in 1522 and converted the Nicarao to Christianity. Spain was chiefly interested in the west. In Granada and Leon, the chief Spanish towns, people farmed and engaged in brisk trade.

In the eighteenth century a Miskito chief gave rights on the east coast to the British, who then held the coast from 1740 to 1786. When the arrangement ended they kept an interest in the place and in 1848 took the port of San Juan del Norte. By that time Nicaragua was an independent state. Spanish rule had ended in 1822 after years of war, and an attempted union with adjacent states ended in 1838.

The east coast went back to Nicaragua in 1860, but there more serious problems arose. In 1912 an unpopular president asked the US to protect him by sending marines. US forces stayed involved with Nicaraguan governments until 1933. After they left, General Somoza of the Nicaraguan National Guard took power in 1937.

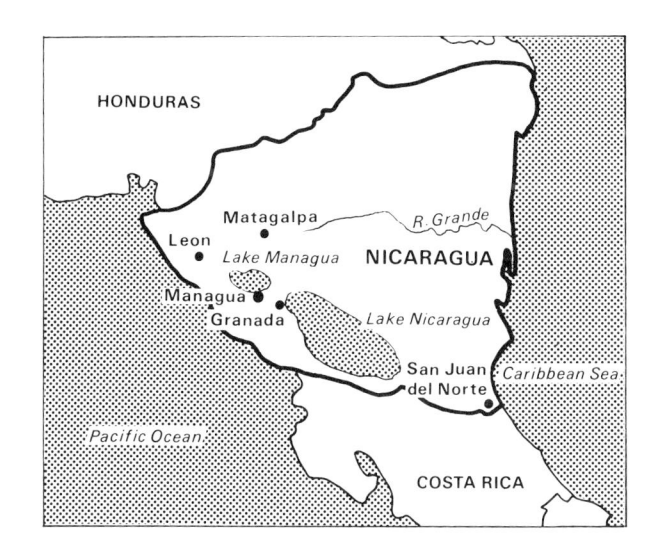

There was so much discontent under Somoza that civil war eventually erupted. In 1979 a new government took office. Nicaragua has suffered greatly from both the war and earthquakes. The west is still farming country. The people speak Spanish, the official language. Most are of mixed Spanish-Nicaraguan descent and Catholics.

Health education for all. Nicaraguan children watch a film on the dangers of insect pests.

JAMAICA

Jamaica is an independent state on an island south of Cuba in the West Indies. The original people were Arawaks, who called the land *Xaymaca,* or "Land of Water."

In 1509 the Spaniards occupied Jamaica, planting sugar and importing African slaves to grow and mill the crop. In 1655 the British took Jamaica in a war. It became a base for British pirates who forced the Spanish planters out.

In the eighteenth century British immigrants arrived — many of them servants who were promised land when their terms as servants was finished. But most plantation work was still done by slaves. There were many slave revolts. Slavery ended in 1834, so new workers were brought in from British colonies in India.

Jamaica used to depend on sugar, and when the price dropped there was great hardship. Many went abroad to find work.

The country became independent in 1962. Most people speak English and are of African descent. Christianity is the main religion; other faiths include Rastafarianism, known for using reggae music.

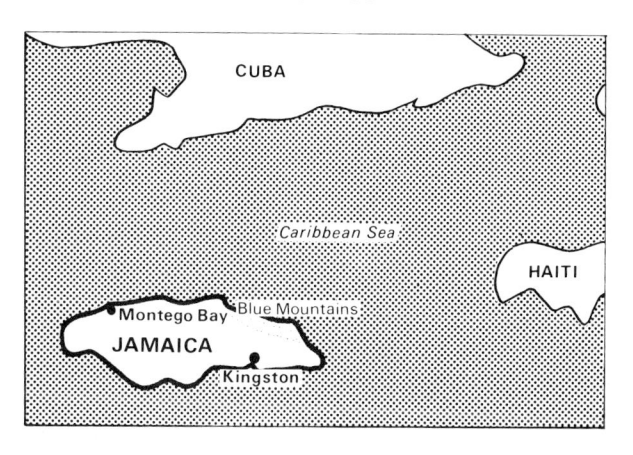

A bustling street market in Costa Rica.

warlords, commoners, and native slaves.

About 1511 Spanish slavers began raiding the Caribbean coast, taking slaves for their new plantations in Cuba. Costa Rica means "Rich Coast," a name invented by Spaniards hoping to tempt merchants with money to invest in the country.

When the country became part of Spanish Central America, most Spanish settlers came to the central valley, west of Turrialba. Despite the "Costa Rica" advertisement, the settlers were not powerful lords or rich merchants. Instead they were simple families coming to work hard and farm their own land.

From 1570 Spanish Central America was ruled from Guatemala, and Costa Rica was not important. Cartago was the only Spanish headquarters until 1700. San José was founded in 1736 and became the capital of Costa Rica in 1823.

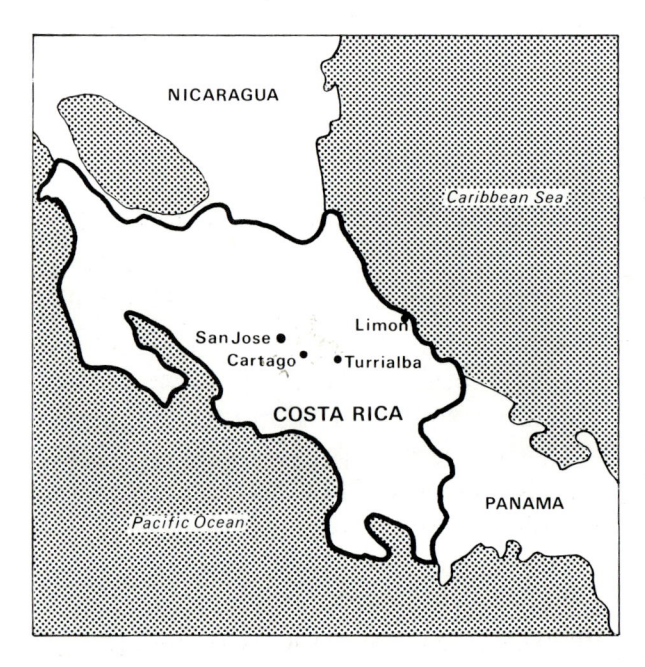

COSTA RICA

Costa Rica is a small Central American republic lying between Nicaragua and Panama. It has a short Caribbean coast and a long Pacific coast. Much of the country is tropical forest, where many of the early people lived, hunted, and fished.

About AD 800 farming people from the south of Mexico invaded the northwest. They were an advanced people, with priests,

There was some cattle ranching in the northwest. On the Caribbean coast, slaves from Africa grew cash crops. Most of the white population lived inland.

Independence from Spain came in 1821. The nineteenth century brought new investment. There were two cash crops for which the market was growing fast — coffee and bananas, both of which were grown by big landowners and big companies. Coffee plantations bought up much of the central valley. US fruit companies had huge banana plantations on the coast. The days of slavery had passed, and the crops were now grown by the slaves' free descendants and by West Indian workers.

Modern Costa Rica has been more peaceful than many Central American nations, but there have been clashes. The big landowners and foreign companies brought in new ideas. The old, self-reliant small farmers have not always agreed with them.

Today most people speak Spanish, are of Spanish descent, and practice the Roman Catholic faith.

PANAMA

Panama is a Central American republic on the narrow isthmus, or bridge of land, that links North and South America. In the middle is an area of lakes where the Panama Canal cuts through the country. On either side, mountains run east and west. There are also regions of hot, humid jungle. The people live mainly on the Pacific coast and in the Canal area.

The early people were the Guaymi in the west and Cuña in the east. Both groups

In Panama today, there are few true-blooded Indians like the two old women above.

farmed by burning off the jungle from small areas at a time or by fishing.

The Spaniards came in the sixteenth century, and Panama became a major part of their American empire. Spanish ships called galleons brought to Panama City all the goods from the west coast, including the great treasures of gold and silver from Peru.

Taboga Island in the Bay of Panama as it looked in the mid-nineteenth century. Today it is a popular tourist resort.

Then the cargos were unloaded and carried across the isthmus to Portobelo. From Portobelo the treasure headed home for Spain, and trade went all around the Caribbean.

In 1739 the British attacked Portobelo and ruined its port. Panama then became a much less important place. In 1751 the Spaniards made Panama part of Colombia.

Attempts to build a canal across Panama began in 1880. But it was low land full of water, exhausting to work in, and full of disease. Years of labor and much money were spent without success.

Then, in 1903, the United States suggested to Colombia that the United States would build a canal from Colon to Balboa. This encouraged the people of Panama to declare themselves independent of Colombia so that they would have all the profit. The US did sign the agreement with Panama instead, and the canal was built. It opened in 1914. The canal brought a large United States population to Panama, for the United States was to control the whole canal area. Today the United States still looks after the canal, but the land around it is once more part of Panama.

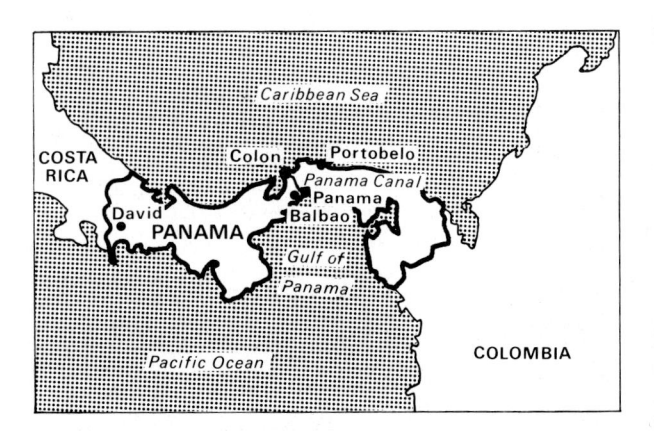

Some Cuña people still live in the east, but most Panamanians are Spanish-speaking, of mixed descent, and Roman Catholic.

CUBA

Cuba is the most northerly state in the West Indies, except for the Bahamas. The main island is long and narrow. Its fertile plains and uplands are broken by mountains at the eastern and western tips as well as in the middle. The Isla de Pinos is part of Cuba.

The early people were mainly Arawaks. They were peaceful village dwellers who were often attacked by Caribs from islands further south.

After 1500 new invaders came. The Spaniards were exploring the West Indies looking for gold and silver, new converts to their Catholic faith, and new subjects for their king and queen. They settled on Cuba, wrongly believing it to be rich in gold. The

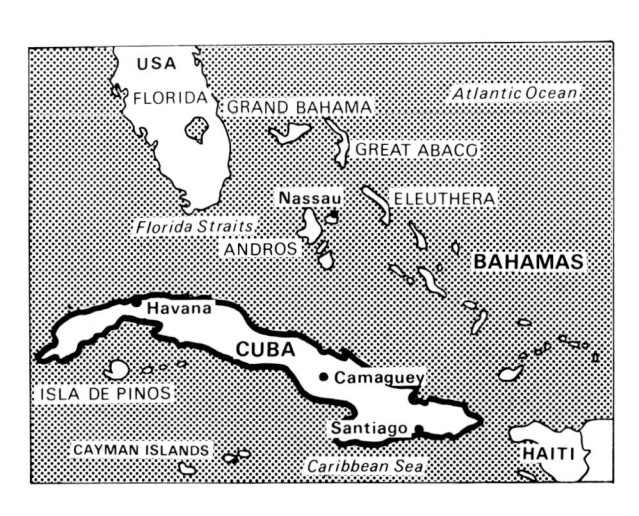

Columbus being greeted by Arawak Indians on his arrival in Cuba in 1492.

Arawaks were forced to mine what little there was, but supplies were soon exhausted. Ambitious Spaniards moved on to Mexico. Those who stayed were primarily interested in cattle ranching, and Arawaks who had survived the mines went back to village life.

Cuba was still useful to Spain, however, because its treasure ships from Mexico sailed home through the Florida Straits. The port and fortress of Havana were built at the southern end of the Straits to protect the fleet. It became a beautiful city in the Spanish style.

Spain showed little interest in the rest of Cuba. The city of Santiago in the east flourished on illegal trading, but Spanish control of Havana's trade was very strict. During the eighteenth century Cubans grew sugar and tobacco, but on a small scale, and all crops had to be sold through Spain.

Havana had a slave trade, but Cubans themselves kept fewer slaves than many West Indian settlers. The climate allowed Europeans to work in the fields, for Cuba lies only just within the tropics.

In 1763 the British occupied Cuba. Their control was brief, but it broke Cuba's trading dependence on Spain. Britain bought

Cuban tobacco and Havana cigars, and Cubans bought slaves more cheaply from British dealers. That enabled them to expand the valuable sugar cane crop.

In the nineteenth century, Cuba's sugar industry made it rich, but Spain now had problems and no longer ruled well. When a war for independence broke out, the United States became anxious about this upheaval so near it, joined in, and defeated Spain. The United States held Cuba from 1899 until 1902. When the occupation ended with Cuba's independence, US control of much Cuban life remained.

In 1959 there was a revolution, and Cuba is now a socialist state. About half the people are of Spanish descent, the rest African and Afro-Spanish. The language is Spanish, the main religion Roman Catholic.

CAYMAN ISLANDS

The Cayman Islands are a British colony in the Caribbean Sea lying between Jamaica and the western tip of Cuba. Grand Cayman, where most people live, is the main island. The others are Little Cayman and Cayman Brac.

The Caymans passed from Spanish to British control in 1670. The islands supplied British seamen with turtle meat. They are still famous for turtles.

Until 1959 the Caymans were part of Jamaica. About half the people are of mixed Afro-European ancestry, English-speaking, and Christian. (See map on page 27.)

Left, a political rally in Cuba shows its support for President Fidel Castro.

Right, sketch of an early encounter between Europeans and the fierce Carib Indians of St. Vincent Island.

THE BAHAMAS

There are about 700 islands and 2,400 islets making up the independent state of the Bahamas. They extend for about 760 miles (475 km) from near southeast Florida to just north of Haiti. The original people were Lucayans, similar to the Arawaks of Haiti. They were destroyed by 1600, mainly by Spanish slave raiders.

After 1648 British settlers came from Bermuda with their African slaves. But pirates became so powerful that at times they ruled. Edward Teach, "Blackbeard," was the most famous pirate. In 1718 the British government sent the first governor to restore order.

The islands were always affected by what was happening in North America, and after the US War of Independence, British colonists came to the Bahamas as refugees. Along with their style of plantation cropping, they brought more slaves. During the US Civil War the Bahamas were a base for blockade running as the tiny islands and narrow sea channels sheltered ships that were supplying the Confederate states, despite the Union's navy patrols.

Today North American visitors make tourism the major industry. English is the official language. Most people are of African descent and practice Christianity. (See map on page 27.)

ST. VINCENT AND THE GRENADINES

St. Vincent is a small island about 100 miles (160 km) west of Barbados. The nearly 600 Grenadine islands run south from it. The northern Grenadines and St. Vincent together make an independent state.

St. Vincent was held by the Carib people until 1763. They were fiercely independent warriors and had no chiefs except as leaders in battle.

From 1763 — except for a French occupation (1779-83) — the British held St. Vincent. But the Caribs often rebelled, and in 1796 they were deported to Roatan Island off the coast of Honduras.

British planters began to develop St. Vincent, but not with big sugar plantations as they did elsewhere in the West Indies. Planters brought in African slaves and grew cotton and arrowroot. When slavery ended they brought in hired workers from India, but few stayed when their contracts ran out.

Mountainous St. Vincent is well forested. The northern peak, La Soufriere, is a volcano that has caused great damage.

The state became independent in 1979. The official language is English, and Protestantism is the main religion. (See map on this page.)

THE TURKS AND CAICOS ISLANDS

These islands are a British colony lying east of Cuba and the Bahamas. In all, they comprise more than thirty small islands, of which only six are inhabited.

British settlers from Bermuda came to the unoccupied islands in 1678 to extract salt. The islands were also used by pirates and smugglers. In 1766 Britain took control, and British refugees from the United States War of Independence, which ended in 1783, came as colonists. From 1874 to 1959 control was transferred to Jamaica. Today most people are Protestant and of African descent. English is the official language. (See map on page 32.)

ANGUILLA

Anguilla is a British colony in the eastern Caribbean Sea. It is the most northern of the Leeward Islands. The smaller island of Sombrero is part of it, together with some tiny islets. They add up to about 35 square miles (91 square km), with about seven thousand people.

The British began to settle people on Anguilla from 1650. They imported slaves from West Africa to work on plantations. Most modern Anguillans are descended from them. The major language is English, and the major religion is Christianity. (See map on this page.)

NETHERLANDS ANTILLES

These six Caribbean islands form an overseas part of the Netherlands. Aruba, Curaçao, and Bonaire lie to the south off the coast of Venezuela, at the western end of the Leeward Islands. Saba, St. Eustatius,

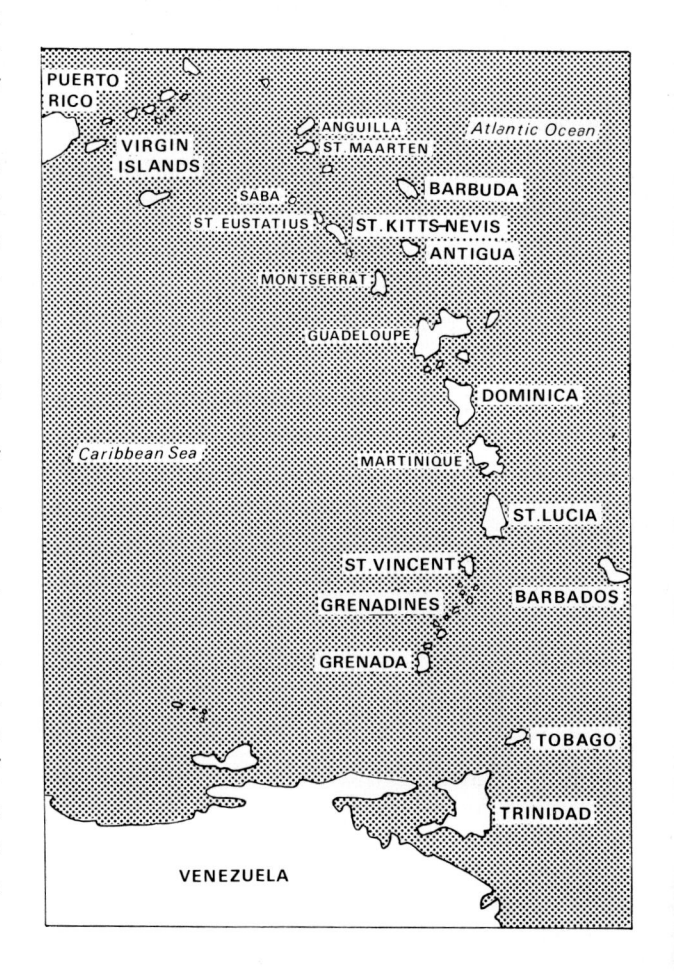

This picture shows the first French settlers who arrived to found the colony of Martinique.

and St. Maarten are in the northern end of the Leeward Islands, at the north end of the Lesser Antilles island chain. The northern half of St. Maarten is owned by Guadeloupe and called by the French name, St. Martin.

The people are of African, American Indian, Dutch, and Spanish descent. Dutch is the official language. People also speak Spanish, English, and Papiamento, a local language derived from the others.

Most people are Roman Catholic, except on St. Eustatius and St. Maarten, where they are mainly Protestant. (See maps on pages 30 and 40.)

MARTINIQUE

Martinique is in the Lesser Antilles island chain, separated from Guadeloupe by Dominica. It is one island, rising to the volcano Mont Pelée, which erupted violently in 1902.

Martinique is an overseas part of France. Like Guadeloupe, it has been French, with short breaks, since 1635.

French is the official language, and people also speak Creole. Most are of African or Afro-French descent. The predominant religion is Roman Catholicism. (See map on page 30.)

BRITISH VIRGIN ISLANDS

These islands are a British dependency lying next door to the US Virgin Islands. There are thirty-six islands. Tortola, where most of the people live, is the biggest. It contains the capital, Road Town.

British sugar planters took over the islands from the Dutch in 1666. Later settlers came as cotton growers or small farmers. The slave trade brought the African population, from which most islanders are descended. The main religion is Protestantism, and the official language English. (See map on page 30.)

UNITED STATES VIRGIN ISLANDS

The islands of St. John, St. Thomas, and St. Croix are territories of the United States. They lie southwest of the Anegada Passage, between the Caribbean Sea and the Atlantic Ocean. The islands were a Danish colony. In 1917 the United States bought the three islands from Denmark.

Most people are of African ancestry and speak US English, but there is a large group from Puerto Rico who speak Spanish. Tourism has replaced sugar cane growing as the chief industry. (See map on page 30.)

The fabulous Palace of Sans Souci, opposite, was built by the first independent king of Haiti between 1804 and 1820. It was later devastated by an earthquake.

HAITI

The republic of Haiti occupies the western end of the island of Hispaniola in the West Indies. The island was settled by Spaniards after 1493. By 1550, the people who had been living there when the Spanish arrived had all died.

The Spaniards lived mainly on the eastern end of Hispaniola. During the seventeenth century, the western end became a refuge for French buccaneers. Buccaneers were escaped convicts, adventurers, shipwrecked sailors, and runaways. Many became pirates, but France found them useful in wartime and protected them. In 1697 it was agreed that western Hispaniola should be a French colony called St. Domingue. Buccaneers settled there to grow sugar, cotton, and coffee.

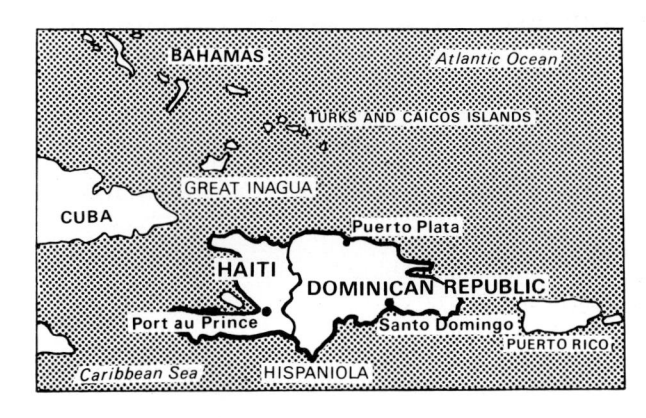

The land was fertile, and French businesspeople invested a lot of money in plantations. More settlers came who later bought African slaves. By 1789 about thirty thousand white settlers lived in Haiti who were French or of French descent. There were 450-500 thousand slaves who were African or of African descent. There were about twenty-seven thousand freed people, mainly mulattos, of mixed racial ancestry. Haitians had an elaborate system of social class based on color and race.

In 1789 a revolution started in France. During and after the French Revolution, the black and mulatto groups in the Haitian colony rebelled. Their revolution brought an end to slavery in Haiti and won the independence of their country from France. This was achieved by a partnership of their class groups, but they found it hard to work together afterward.

The new state of Haiti still had many social classes. The lightest mulattos soon replaced the white plantation owners at the top. Black groups were divided between those long settled in Haiti, those of French culture, and the newly arrived immigrants. French-speaking, Roman Catholic black Haitians did not follow popular African customs and beliefs, such as the voodoo religion, for example.

Rival groups got foreign support and encouraged foreign investment. French, British, German, and Syrian businesses opened in the cities. The most interested foreign country was the United States, to whom Haiti was soon deeply in debt.

US military forces occupied Haiti from 1915 until 1934. They did not recognize all the differences of color Haitians did, so those with the darkest skin were equal to light-skinned people. Many people of color grew up with a strong interest in their African culture, rejecting European ideas, politics, and religion. François Duvalier shared this interest. He took power and named himself President of Haiti in 1958. The Duvalier family ruled Haiti until 1986, when they were overthrown. Haiti's official language is French. Creole patois, a dialect, ia also widely spoken. Roman Catholicism and voodoo are the main religions. (See map on page 32.)

GRENADA

Grenada is a small state, a tiny island north of Trinidad united with the southern Grenadine islands. The early people of Grenada were Caribs who had come north from the Orinoco basin of South America.

The French settled on Martinique, to the north, in the seventeenth century. They tried to buy Grenada. The Caribs refused to sell the island, so the French attacked. Grenada was French until 1762 when the British took over. The French won it back in 1779, but the British regained it for good in 1783.

Grenada was planted with spices, and slaves were brought from West Africa. In the nineteenth century slavery ended in Grenada. Hired workers from India replaced the slave labor.

Grenada became independent in 1974. There are still some French dialects in use, and half the people are Roman Catholic, like the original French settlers, but the official language is English. (See map on page 30.)

DOMINICAN REPUBLIC

The Dominican Republic is the eastern and larger part of the island of Hispaniola in the West Indies. The Spaniards made a settlement there in 1492, at La Isabela, west of Puerto Plata. They found peaceful Arawaks ruled by local chiefs, who farmed and fished for a living. In far eastern Hispaniola lived the fierce Caribs. In the end neither tribal group survived Spanish occupation very long.

Spanish settlers died of tropical diseases or were killed by hurricanes. Arawaks died of European diseases brought by settlers and from being forced to work at hard labor for the Europeans.

After 1500 the Spaniards began to grow sugar cane. They invested in mills to crush the cane and bought African slaves to do the work in the fields. By 1550 the Arawaks and Caribs had largely died out, but the number of West Africans was growing.

The colony was not rich and was often attacked by pirates. A colony of French pirates had control of western Hispaniola by 1697. Spain then agreed that western Hispaniola should be French — what is now Haiti. The Spanish part became known as Santo Domingo.

Sugar growing and cattle raising flourished, and many more Spanish settlers arrived after 1740.

In 1795, Spain ceded the land to France but regained control in 1809. Spanish rule was not sound but they regained the title to Santo Domingo in 1814, and in 1821 the island declared its independence. It was occupied by Haiti until the independent Dominican Republic was founded in 1844.

The new republic was anxious for the protection of some powerful foreign state, to keep the Haitians out. But many black Dominicans were in favor of Haiti, which had a majority of black people. Ambitious people made the most of the disagreements, and there was frequent civil war.

By 1905 the country was bankrupt, and the United States took control of its revenue. Since then, the United States has been influential in the Dominican Republic's history.

Today most people are of Spanish or Afro-Spanish descent and speak Spanish. The main faith is Roman Catholicism. (See map on page 32.)

This engraving shows the Bay of Samana in Hispaniola during the 1860s. In earlier days coves like this one provided shelter for pirates, buccaneers, and other adventurers.

ST. LUCIA

St. Lucia is an independent state on a small, volcanic island. It is one of the Windward Islands, which are the easternmost group of islands in the West Indies. Its two peaks called the Pitons have long been landmarks for sailors as they headed out of the Atlantic towards the Caribbean Sea.

The original Carib people of St. Lucia were defeated by European settlers, after holding out for a long time. The island was settled by the French and the British and claimed by both. St. Lucia finally passed to Britain in 1814.

Despite the British claim, most people are of French or Afro-French descent, and French dialects are spoken, although the official language is English. The main church is the Roman Catholic Church, which the French introduced.

St. Lucia was a plantation island and still grows sugar cane, cocoa, and fruit. (See map on page 30.)

ANTIGUA AND BARBUDA

This small state is made up of three islands: Antigua, Barbuda, and Redonda. They lie in the eastern Leeward Islands of the Caribbean Sea. About eighty thousand people live on Antigua and Barbuda. Nobody lives on Redonda.

Columbus gave Antigua its Spanish name in 1493. The first European settlers, however, were English. Around 1632 they began to grow sugar cane and cotton. They brought slaves from West Africa to do the planting and harvesting.

The territory became a British colony in which most people were of African descent. Now independent of Britain, the state keeps the English language and English forms of Christianity. (See map on page 30.)

MONTSERRAT

Montserrat is a very small island of the Lesser Antilles.

It is a British colony. Irish and English Catholics settled there beginning in 1632. They grew tobacco and sugar cane using African slave labor. British possession was made certain in 1783.

By that time there were — and still are — more people of African than of European descent.

The official language is English. There are now more Protestants than Catholics. (See map on page 30.)

Although Antigua was settled by the British, many of its buildings, like the church opposite, reflect a Spanish heritage.

Like many Central and South American countries, Barbados is famous for colorful celebrations like the one at right.

PUERTO RICO

Puerto Rico is the farthest east of the large Caribbean islands, which are called the Greater Antilles. It is a territory of the United States, and it includes the small islands of Vieques, Culebra, and Mona.

Puerto Rico began as a Spanish colony, first settled in 1508. It fell to the United States in 1898, after the Spanish-American War, becoming a US territory.

The people speak Spanish and US English. They are of European and African descent, and many are Roman Catholic. (See map on page 32.)

BARBADOS

Barbados is a very small island, the farthest east of the West Indies. It lies in the Atlantic Ocean northeast of Trinidad.

No one lived there when Britain colonized it in 1627. The land was flat, dry, and good for growing sugar cane.

British sugar cane plantation owners brought in slaves, mainly from West Africa. The planters built large, handsome houses. Barbados traded with English colonies in North America and grew rich.

Less wealthy settlers were Scottish war prisoners who had been sent to Barbados by the English government after 1651.

Barbados became very crowded, and every inch of land was used. Slavery ended in 1834, but there was nowhere for freed slaves to farm on their own. Most stayed on plantations, so labor was still plentiful and wages were very low.

Barbados remained British until 1966 when it became an independent state. Today most people are of African descent, and speak English. Most are members of Protestant religions. (See map on page 30.)

ST. KITTS-NEVIS

Together, the two small islands of St. Kitts, or St. Christopher's, and Nevis form a country. They lie near the northern end of the Lesser Antilles island chain.

St. Kitts was colonized first. British settlers came in 1623 and French settlers in 1625. The British moved on to Nevis in 1628. Nevis had poor soil, but St. Kitts had rich, volcanic soil. The French hung on to parts of St. Kitts until 1712.

The first English settlers were not rich planters. Some were ex-servants. Some were artisans and small landholders. They were prey to tropical diseases, earthquakes, and hurricanes. Their small farms grew tobacco, indigo, and spices. Slave traders brought in African slaves to sell, but the farmers could not afford to buy many. Sugar cane planting came later, and then the big estates with many slaves became very common.

Slaves were freed on both islands in 1834. The islands were united in 1882 and became independent in 1983. The people are English-speaking and mainly of African descent, with various Christian faiths. (See map on page 30.)

DOMINICA

Dominica is a small country in the Lesser Antilles. The island is mountainous and wet. It is the most northerly of the Windward Islands.

The Caribs were the first people in Dominica, and some still live there. They used to be warriors and cannibals. Caribs were great canoeists, and probably used canoes to travel up the Antilles island chain from the coast of South America.

France bought land from the Caribs and slowly won control of Dominica in the seventeenth century, but after war with Britain, they passed Dominica to the British in 1763.

The island grows splendid fruit, but the rain and the mountains make it less suitable for sugar cane plantations. Some slaves were imported, however, and the people are now mainly of African or mixed descent.

Dominica became an independent state in 1978. English is the official language, but local dialects and customs are still French. Roman Catholicism is the main religion. (See map on page 30.)

GUADELOUPE

Guadeloupe is an overseas colony of France. It has been French, with short breaks, since the mid-seventeenth century.

There are seven islands that make up Guadeloupe. Five are at the south end of the Leeward Islands and two — St. Barthélemy and St. Martin — lie at the north end of the group.

People speak French, the official language, and Creole, a French dialect. Most are of African or Afro-French descent. St. Barthélemy and Les Saints are still home to descendants of seventeenth-century settlers from Brittany and Normandy in France. Roman Catholicism is the main religion. (See map on page 30.)

TRINIDAD AND TOBAGO

Trinidad and Tobago are two islands that make up one republic. They are close to the northern coast of South America, opposite the delta of the Orinoco River, which was the homeland of their original people. They were Caribs, a warlike race. When European explorers arrived there was fighting with the Caribs. Eventually, the Dutch won Tobago and the Spaniards won Trinidad. French settlement came later. Both islands had became British colonies by 1802.

Trinidad had fewer African slaves then many of the other islands had, and when the British banned the slave trade in 1833, the settlers could not import more.

There were some islanders of African descent, some Spaniards, and French refugees from the French Revolution, which had affected French islands as much as it had France. The British hired Indian workers to replace the slaves. They also brought in Chinese workers, but the Indians settled in larger numbers.

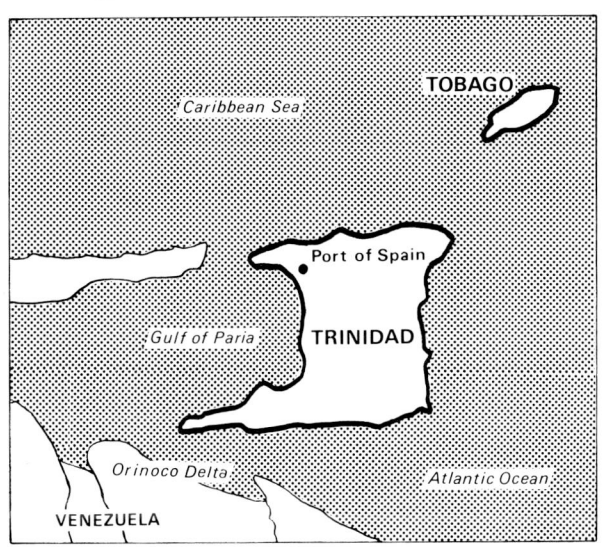

The islands became independent in 1962. Today, about 40% of the people are of African descent and 40% are Indian. The rest are of European, Chinese, or mixed ancestry. The official language is English. The biggest religious groups are Roman Catholics and Hindus.

VENEZUELA

Venezuela is a republic on the northern coast of South America. Western Venezuela reaches the northern end of the Andes Mountains. There are other highlands along the coast, and the Guyana Mountains rise in the southeast. Central Venezuela is the *llanos* — grassy plains watered by the Orinoco river.

The early people of Venezuela had farming villages in the coastal hills. They were also able to farm in the Guyana jungles, where they cleared small plots of ground by burning vegetation. Elsewhere they hunted or fished. They lived in small groups ruled by local chiefs.

The Spaniards settled Venezuela in the sixteenth century. They came from their bases in the Caribbean Islands. From there they found the pearl fisheries off the Venezuelan coast. Then they came inland, looking for slaves, gold, and copper. It was some time before they began to settle as crop growers, and then their conquest of the country became very slow.

Small towns were founded in the Andes Mountains and around Lake Maracaibo. The Spaniards used local people as labor, and many of these laborers adapted to the Spanish way of life. There was also a settlement at Caracas. In 1580 smallpox

A lonely residence on the banks of one of the Amazon River's many tributaries.

destroyed the local farming villages around Caracas. This enabled the settlers in Caracas to spread out over the land. Caracas itself had a healthy climate for Europeans, but Lake Maracaibo did not. Caracas became the most important city.

In 1728 the Caracas Company was founded by Basque merchants from northern Spain. The company laid out plantations of cacao and bought African slaves. The industry did well, and the Basques became a powerful group in Venezuela. Other Spanish settlers came from the Spanish colony of the Canary Islands.

By 1800 there was a mixed racial and ethnic population. More than half of the Venezuelans were of African descent, working as slaves in plantations or in Spanish households. Native Venezuelans still hunted and fished in the Orinoco Delta and the thickly forested southern hills. Natives of the north had either mingled with the

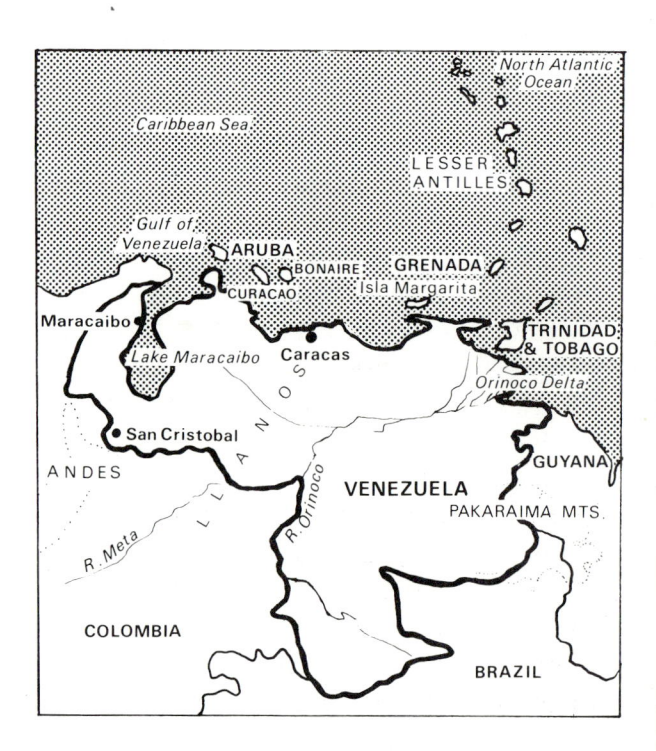

Spaniards or run away from the colonizers into the llanos.

The llanos were also a refuge for runaway slaves, outlaws, and mestizos or people of mixed Spanish and Indian ancestry. Cattle ranchers used these men as cowboys, looking after herds that were half wild. The only towns in the llanos grew from Catholic missions, where Franciscan, Jesuit, and other missionaries worked among cowboys and local tribes.

Many successful people lived in the north, especially in Caracas. Their society was stratified by class, from Spanish-born at the top down to black slave. Llanos men did not belong in the class system anywhere. They were resentful of the class system, and ready for rebellion.

A war of independence from Spain began in 1810 and became a civil war as well. At first Spanish forces used the llanos cowboys against rich landowners who wanted independence. But in 1817 the cowboys were won over by Simón Bolívar, leader of the independence movement. By 1824 the Spanish side had lost, and Venezuela became a republic, united with Colombia. That union ended in 1829. Venezuela broke away and the cowboys' leader, José Antonio Páez, became the first president. Llanos leaders were rewarded with ranches and became even more powerful.

From then on there was often trouble between the merchants of the north and the llanos dictators with private armies.

In 1914 oil was found. Venezuela had become the world's biggest exporter of oil by 1929. Oil brought wealth and many immigrants to the nation. The last *caudillo*, or dictator, was overthrown in 1958.

Most of the people are of mixed Spanish and native Indian descent, and are Roman Catholics. Many Indian dialects are spoken in Venezuela as well as the official language, Spanish.

ARUBA

Aruba is an island off the coast of Venezuela. It is a self-governing dependency of the Netherlands.

Aruba was settled by Arawak people from South America. Spain claimed it in 1499. It became Dutch in 1634, but only as a garrison. Settlement spread only recently because of the gold-mining and oil industries that have developed.

Half the modern Arubans are of mixed Arawak and Dutch heritage. Others are of Spanish, Indian, and Chinese descent. (See map on page 40.)

BOLIVIA

Bolivia is a landlocked country in central South America, lying between Argentina and Brazil. Western Bolivia is mountainous. There are two parallel ranges of the Andes, with a high plateau between them, where the air is thin and hard to breathe. This plateau is called the Altiplano, and it is where most of western Bolivia's people live. Eastern Bolivia is lowland tropical forest in the Amazon River basin. It is savanna elsewhere.

The Altiplano has always been the most important region. There, close to the great Lake Titicaca, was an early state of mountain people who conquered parts of Peru around AD 600. They spoke Quechua and

The Indians of Bolivia fish Lake Titicaca today as they have for centuries. Here a woman awaits the return of her husband, who is fishing.

Aymara languages. Their prosperity came from farming, but those south of the lake had a city at Tiahuanaco.

Farming in the Andes can be very successful. Small plots can grow the family's vegetables and grain. Llamas are used as pack animals and for meat and fleece. Alpacas have an even better fleece. Both animals thrive in the high mountains.

Spaniards came to Bolivia in the sixteenth century seeking silver and gold. The Altiplano was then part of the Inca empire. The Spaniards conquered the Inca empire and replaced its efficient organization with their own. They brought many Roman Catholic monks and friars to convert the Inca to Christianity.

In Bolivia the Spaniards found the biggest source of silver in South America. The mountain of Potosí was full of silver. The mines were opened in 1545. But Potosí stood fifteen thousand feet above sea level, and Spaniards could live only for short periods of time in thin air.

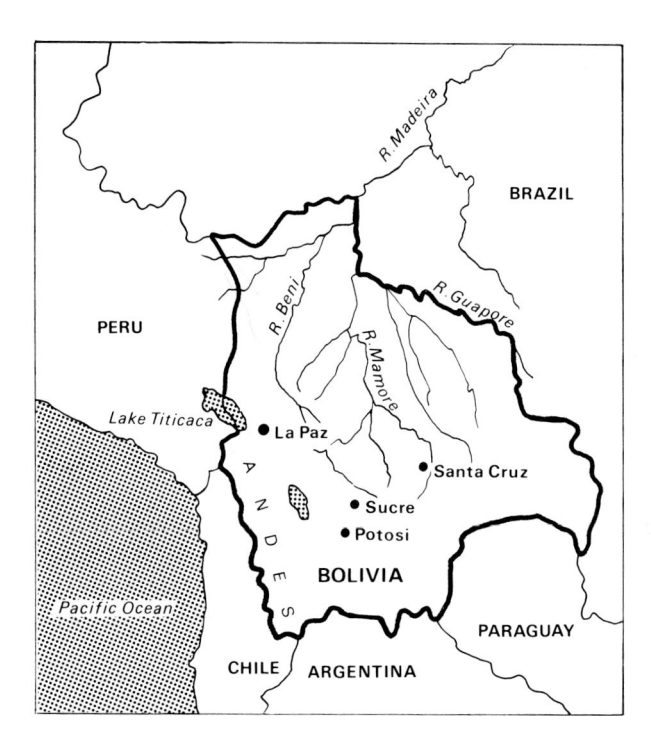

Spanish families did not settle in Potosí. To mine the silver they used their new subjects whom they had won from the Inca emperor. Thousands of Bolivians were sent to work in the mines. They made the new city of Potosí very splendid. Great llama trains and mule trains of goods crossed the Andes to supply it with corn and meat. Potosí was famous throughout the Spanish empire, but it was a place from which the mine owners departed as soon as they had made their fortunes. During the eighteenth century the silver ran out and the city died. The mountain people went back to farming. Spaniards who stayed in Bolivia went down to the lower slopes of the Andes to establish their estates.

Eastern Bolivia was not much affected

by Spanish rule. Jungle tribes still lived near the Amazon River. In the south was a lowland called the Chaco, where a fierce people lived by raiding other people. When the Spaniards came the Chaco raiders stole their horses, learned how to master them, and were then able to raid farther and faster than before.

Bolivia was ruled as Upper Peru until the country became independent as a republic in 1825. General Antonio José de Sucré defeated the Spaniards, and Bolivia was named after his commander, Simón Bolívar. Bolivia, like some other South American states, kept the Spanish tradition of a strong, central ruler supported by powerful landowners. There were quarrels between these different groups and civil war resulted.

Since 1900 the country has lived primarily by exporting tin mined in the Andes. In recent years, oil has been found too. Bolivia has lost control of a lot of land in war, including its coast. Bolivia has been trying to make the most of what is left by settling newcomers to develop the eastern lowland. Japanese colonists began farming there as early as 1908.

Today the mountain people with their small farms make up most of the population. They still speak Quechua and Aymara. The Chaco people speak Guaraní. Spanish is the official language and Roman Catholicism is the main religion.

URUGUAY

Uruguay is a small South American republic on the north side of the Rio de la Plata estuary. The country is grassland, and on the coast is the big port of Montevideo, which is also the capital and largest city.

The earliest known people were the Charruas, a warlike race who fought against European settlement. Not until 1726 was Montevideo founded by the Spanish rulers of Buenos Aires, Argentina. At that time there were Spanish settlements along the Rio de la Plata. Far to the north in Brazil there were colonies of Portuguese. In Uruguay itself there were Spanish cattle ranchers looking for new pastures. There were smugglers from the rich mines of the Andes, heading for the coast. The area had no strong government, and cattle raiding was widespread and frequent.

The great cattle ranches of Brazil were mainly in the north. In 1791-93 they suffered a severe drought, partly induced by reckless clearing of woodland to make way for cattle. The ranchers were forced south with their surviving herds. They came to the Rio Grande do Sul province, just north of

Uruguay. Uruguay itself they called the Banda Oriental. It was a frontier between themselves and Argentina. As Brazilian ranchers spread, they moved into the Banda Oriental. In time they came to believe that it ought to be part of Brazil. By then, however, small towns had been founded by Spanish immigrants from the Buenos Aires region of Argentina.

In 1822 Brazil became an independent country and claimed the Banda Oriental as its own. Montevideo was such an important cattle port and the grazing land was so rich that Argentina disputed Brazil's claim at once. In 1825 they invaded the country and drove the Brazilians out. In 1828, the people decided to solve the dispute by making the Banda Oriental an independent country. The name Uruguay was the river between the new state and Argentina.

Uruguay has a temperate climate that suited European farmers. The independent country received many new settlers, mostly from Spain and Italy. They continued the farming of cattle and sheep, exporting their meat from Montevideo.

Uruguay was a place of small and medium-sized ranches and sheep farms. The ranchers and farmers were not like the powerful owners of millions of acres who tried to control governments and other people in nearby states.

After 1903 Uruguay had a type of welfare state, founded by President José Batlle y Ordónez. This attracted many more Europeans, and there has been further immigration since.

The official language of Uruguay is Spanish. The country's predominant religion is Roman Catholicism.

In the picture opposite three Colombian musicians, dressed in traditional costumes, take a break during a performance.

COLOMBIA

Colombia is a republic at the northwest tip of South America. It has a Pacific coast and a Caribbean coast with the isthmus of Panama in between. The isthmus was part of Colombia between 1821 and 1903.

Colombia is tropical, but the Andes Mountains offer cooler air, and most of the people live there. The early people included the Chocó, who hunted and fished on the Pacific Coast, and the Chibcha in the Andes. The Chibcha were clever, and some of their farming villages became rich enough to grow into towns, each with its own ruler. They were also famous for doing excellent work with gold.

In the sixteenth century the Spaniards conquered Mexico and parts of Central America. Finding gold was one of their main ambitions. They heard of a town near Bogotá, where the ruler covered himself in gold dust for religious festivals. They called him El Dorado, which means "The Gilded Man." They came into Colombia to find him and, in time, gained control of the coast and the mountains. They called the place New Granada.

After 1550 the Spaniards found a rich gold mine in the Cauca Valley. Later, they found more gold in the hills of Antioquia. Many local people were forced to work in the mines. The port of Cartagena was built to ship the gold back to Spain. There were great guns to defend the treasure ships.

On the tropical coast, the Spaniards planted cash crops. Most of the work was done by slaves imported from West Africa. The Chibcha laborers were dying of European diseases. Survivors escaped to the jungles beyond the Andes, where white men could not live.

There were some small communities of miners working their own claims who could not get Chibcha labor and could not afford slaves. They had to be hard-working and energetic. Their main area was Antioquia, which turned out to be good land for growing coffee. Many more people adopted the new crop in the nineteenth century. Those who did well put their money into new industries at Medellín.

By that time New Granada was independent after a civil war. From 1819 until 1830 the country embraced Venezuela and Ecuador. It became a single republic in

In Colombia school is not just for children. Here pupils of all ages enter their classroom for a lesson taught to them on the radio.

1830 and was named The United States of Colombia in 1863.

Wealthy men still invested in big plots of land. There was rivalry between them and the businesspeople of Medellín, which sometimes led to civil war. There was much upheaval until around 1910. After that, coffee made Colombia much richer and more stable for a while. The old rivalries flared up again in 1946, and there has been further unrest since. Colombia is like many South American states: country people who have no land move to the cities, only to find that there is no work that they are able to do. Much of the country is jungle that cannot be developed to easily solve the problem of creating jobs.

Colombia still has gold, emeralds, and other precious minerals and continues to grow coffee. There is cattle ranching in the northeast. Most people are of mixed racial and ethnic descent. The main language is Spanish, and the predominant faith in the country is Roman Catholicism.

FRENCH GUIANA

French Guiana belongs to France. It lies on the northeastern coast of South America. The early French settlers were planters, growing their crops near the coast using the labor of African slaves. Some white settlers also came as laborers before they gained their own small farms.

When slavery was abolished, many plantations failed. Some areas became convict settlements, Devil's Island being the best known. Prisoners were all removed by the early 1950s.

Most French Guianans are of French, African, or mixed ancestry, practice the Roman Catholic faith, and speak French. Minority tribal groups continue to live in the forests. (See map on page 47.)

SURINAME

Suriname lies between Guyana and French Guiana on the northeastern coast of South America. It was one of the Guianas explored by French, Dutch, and British trading companies in the seventeenth century. Guiana was a local word meaning water. Suriname is bounded and divided by rivers. It is a hot, wet country.

A Spanish explorer found the coast in 1499. Arawak tribes lived there, raided by fiercer Caribs moving along the coast.

In 1644 Dutch and Portuguese settlers came to the Suriname River to grow sugar cane. A British colony nearby was destroyed by Caribs in 1645 and revived in 1650. It was a business investment that had to make a strong profit.

The British copied the Dutch and Portuguese methods of growing sugar cane. All plantations used the labor of West African slaves. The plantations grew rich.

In 1667 it was agreed that Suriname should belong to the Dutch, and it became Dutch Guiana until 1975. In return for giving up their colony, the British received a Dutch colony in North America called New Netherland. Suriname's sugar exports were so valuable that the British thought they had lost badly on the exchange. However, New Netherland became New York State.

In the eighteenth century, many slaves were running away from the plantations. They banded together in the forests, making colonies of their own. They were called Bush Negroes, or Maroons. Some became very strong — planters tried in vain to conquer them.

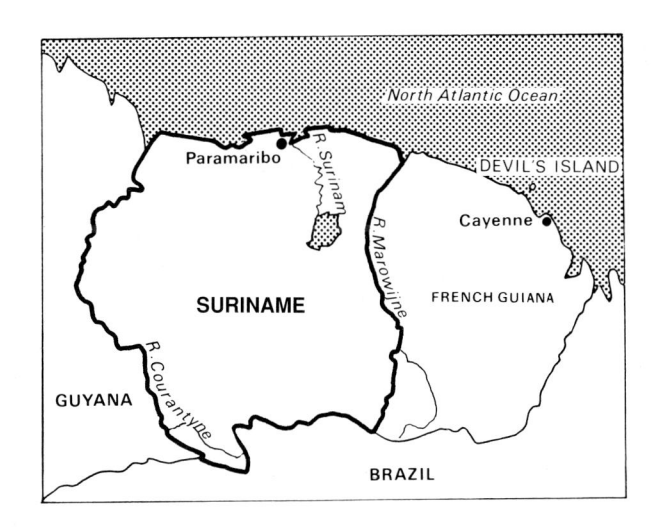

In the nineteenth century slavery ended in Suriname. The Dutch then encouraged immigration from their other colonies in the Far East. Indians, Chinese, and Javanese arrived to take the slaves' places on the plantations as paid labor. They brought new faiths — Islam and Hinduism — to join the Protestant Christianity of the Dutch.

In 1975 Suriname became an independent republic. A military government took control in 1980. The official language is Dutch, although English, Hindi, Javanese, and Chinese are also used.

BRAZIL

Brazil is an enormous country. It shares frontiers with every state of South America except Ecuador and Chile.

The northwestern quarter of Brazil is the Amazon region. This river basin has mountains, jungle, and dense forest. It is hot and humid. Forest and jungle used to cover most of Brazil, and the early people lived in this harsh climate.

Jungle nomads speaking Tupi and Tapuya languages moved through the forests hunting and fishing. They worshipped the spirits in nature. Many believed in a great spirit who would lead them to a paradise. In the sixteenth century, the Tupinambas undertook a nine-year journey to the Andes, looking for their promised land.

At the same time Portuguese colonists

Brazil is home to many different tribes. In the depths of the Amazon jungle Indians like those in the picture above still live by hunting and fishing.

came to the coast. They wanted profitable cargo for their merchant ships. At first they traded in fine timber from the forests. Later they made sugar plantations on the coast. In the 1690s, about the time sugar stopped being profitable, miners discovered gold in Minas Gerais. After the gold ran out, settlers moved south to grow coffee or to breed cattle. There was even more cattle land in the north. The jungle trees yielded rubber. The center of activity was always moving in Brazil. Settling was always done by going into new regions for new kinds of business. At the same time people moved away from places they had exhausted. Even though the farmers and settlers were from many nations, Portugal eventually came to control the whole country.

The government was not anxious to conquer the nomadic tribes or to help the Christian missionaries convert them, but some of the settlers hunted for slaves. Catholic priests then tried to protect the victims. There was often trouble between farming settlers and jungle tribes. The settlers could win only by burning down the jungle, leaving their attackers without cover.

There was peaceful contact too, and in time the races mixed.

The slave hunters had been trying to supply labor for plantations on the coast but could never supply enough. Portugal already had trading bases in West Africa, where Portuguese dealers bought slaves from local chiefs. These slaves were now shipped across to Brazil. More than three million slaves had arrived by 1800. Not all of them remained slaves. Some were freed to become traders or artisans. Some escaped to a hard life in remote country. Some married into Portuguese families.

In 1822 Brazil became independent of Portugal but with a Portuguese emperor. At that time the slave trade was dying. Foreign navies prevented the slave ships from reaching Brazilian ports, so the settlers began once more to exploit the jungle and enslave forest people.

Brazil became a republic in 1889, with Portuguese as the official language. There was then a population of Portuguese, native Indian, African, and mixed descent. The southeast became crowded. São Paulo was the center of the coffee industry. Rio de Janeiro was the capital. Farther south were cattle ranches and farms. There was still mining in Minas Gerais, but other metals had replaced gold. In the northwest the

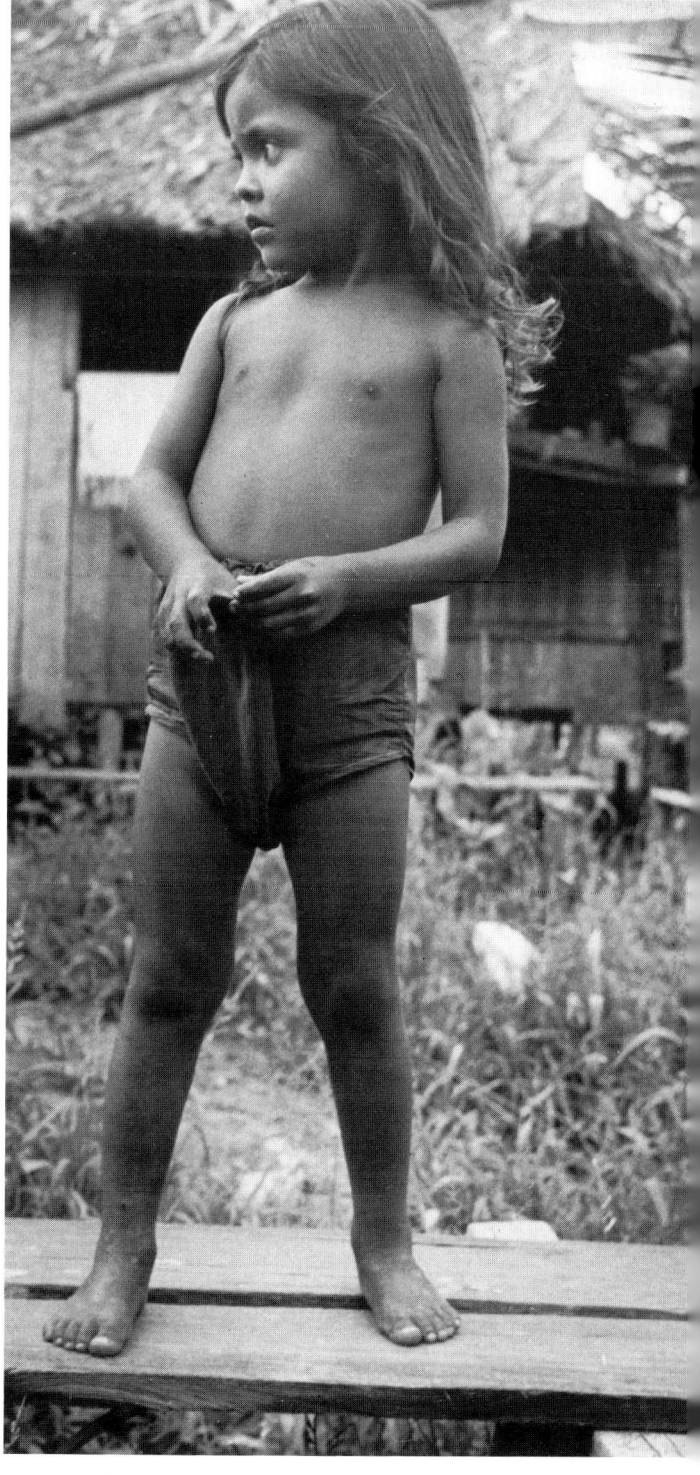

The slums of the "vila da barcas," where this girl lives, are built on stilts to avoid the tides of the Amazon River.

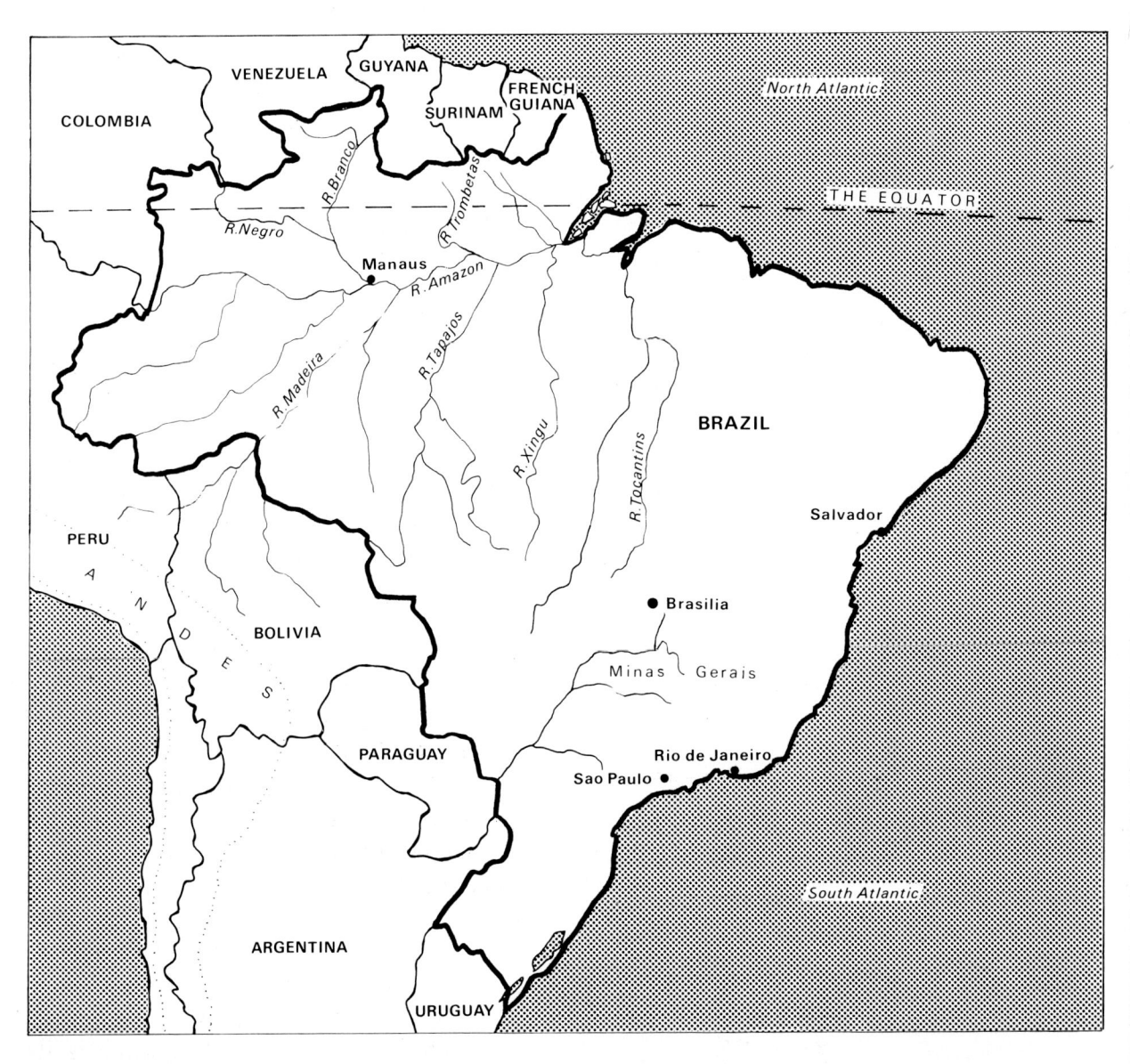

tropical forest was producing rubber, and there was a trading city, Manaus, on the Amazon River.

Brazil has great riches and great poverty. There have been plans to resettle country people who have no land. Forests have been cleared for small farming, but forest tribes are unable to live anywhere else but in their forest. The new capital of Brasília has been built on the central plateau, well inland from Rio de Janeiro.

About half of all South Americans live in Brazil, and about half the Brazilians live in the southeastern part of the country. Roman Catholicism is the predominant religion, and Portuguese is the official language. Brazil's Afro-American character is probably best known through music and dance.

GUYANA

Guyana is a republic on the northeastern coast of South America. The country lies along important rivers — the Cuyuni, Mazaruni, Essequibo, Demerara, and Berbice.

The rivers first attracted Dutch explorers looking for trading bases. There were small Dutch settlements on the coast by 1613, and in 1616, the Dutch founded an important trading post at Bartica. There the Dutch traded with Arawak tribes for slaves, who were usually prisoners of war, and for other goods. In 1686 the settlers were forbidden to enslave free tribespeople. When settlers founded big sugar estates on the coast, they ran out of labor and began importing West African slaves.

The Dutch were used to reclaiming coastal land in their own country. But in order to do well with sugar in Guyana, they had to reclaim on a very big scale. In 1716 they opened the country to foreign settlers, hoping to attract enough investors for the new estates. Many of the new planters were British, from Britain's many island colonies in the Caribbean.

After 1791 there was a time of confusion. The British and Dutch were on opposite sides in a European war at home. British colonists had become very strong in Guyana. They wanted British rule and got it in 1814. Guyana was named British Guiana. Dutch law and a Dutch style of government remained until 1928, however, when British colonial government was imposed.

The slaves were freed in 1834, but nobody had worked out how they could fit into the new economy. Social class was based on color with white planters at the top, and free blacks at the bottom. Land was too expensive for them to buy, and many of their former jobs went to workers hired from India and China.

Energetic freed slaves stopped growing crops and became traders. Indians began a rice-growing industry. There was a gold rush in the 1880s, and in 1914 the country began to produce bauxite, which is used in making aluminum. All of these things helped to counterbalance the power of the sugar planters. British rule ended in 1966.

Modern Guyana is a republic, with fierce political rivalry between groups of Indian and African descent. English is the official language; Hindi and Urdu are also widely used. Most people practice the Hindu or Christian religions.

PARAGUAY

Paraguay is a small, landlocked South American republic that has borders with Brazil, Bolivia, and Argentina. The Paraguay River crosses the country from north to south, and provides the fertile land where most people live. West of the river is the Gran Chaco — a plain of scrub woodland. East of the river, the land rises sharply to forested hills.

The early people, who are still there, were the Guaraní. Their name means "warriors" but they also hunted, fished, and grew food.

In 1537 the Spaniards, who were then rulers of Peru, made a colony in Paraguay. They had discovered the country by traveling upriver from the Rio de la Plata estuary. They had settlements on the estuary and they thought the river would lead them to silver-bearing mountains in the Andes. In fact they got no farther than the site of Asunción. There was arid country ahead and hostile Guaraní.

Spanish missionaries, especially the Jesuits after 1568, worked and settled among the Guaraní. Their Christian teaching was similar to some ideas the Guaraní already had: that a leader from God would take them to a peaceful, promised land. Guaraní who became Christians were brought to live in villages around missions, where Jesuits encouraged good farming.

Until 1767 Paraguay was part of Spanish Peru, and Peru had economic control. But in that year there were two changes. Paraguay became part of a new province based on the Rio de la Plata, with the right to export its own goods through Asunción. The Jesuits were turned out of Spanish America, and their lands were offered for sale. This made Paraguay more attractive to Spanish settlers, and less safe for Guaraní. Many escaped into the forest.

Paraguay became independent of Spain in 1811. The dominant settlers, however, carried on the Spanish style of strong, central government. In 1865-70, Paraguay fought Argentina, Brazil, and Uruguay. Paraguay wanted power over the whole river network flowing into the Rio de la Plata but lost the war.

Paraguay won the Chaco war against Bolivia in 1932-35 but lost many soldiers. Foreign settlers were encouraged, including Japanese, Koreans, and Germans.

Today most Paraguayans are Roman Catholics of mixed Spanish-Guaraní descent. Half the population is bilingual. Only a few speak just Spanish.

Here a group of llamas graze peacefully in sight of Mount Cotopaxi in central Ecuador, the highest active volcano in the world.

ECUADOR

Ecuador is a small republic on the Pacific coast of South America, between Colombia and Peru. The state includes the Galápagos Islands. Mainland Ecuador has a narrow plain along the coast. Behind are the Andes Mountains and beyond them lies the jungle.

The jungles and river valleys have many small groups of people, each with many languages. The Andes people speak Quechua, the language of the Incas of Peru.

The Incas had taken Ecuador into their empire by 1500. They built the city of Quito as their capital, on the slopes of the great volcano Pichincha. The surrounding people kept small farms.

In 1532 the Inca empire fell to Spain. Quito became a Spanish headquarters. From there, Spanish Catholic missionaries moved out on to the mountains. They were Jesuits, skilled estate managers, and farmers. They had sheep farms in the Andes and used the profits for mission work. There were few other Spanish settlers. Some tried to grow cotton with local forced labor, but the people rebelled. Other cash-crop plantations on the coast employed African slaves.

The Jesuit missions explored far into the jungle, toward the Amazon River. This area is now part of Peru, but Ecuador has always claimed it. Many of the settlements began as missions, set up by Jesuits from Quito.

Ecuador gained freedom from Spain between 1809 and 1821. It was Simón Bolívar of Venezuela and his marshal, Sucré, who defeated the Spanish forces. Bolívar then persuaded Ecuador to be united with Venezuela and Colombia. But the union was not popular, and ended in 1830 with Ecuador as an independent republic.

The coast is still farmed as plantations on which cacao, bananas, coffee, and sugar grow. The Andes have the most comfortable climate because Ecuador lies on its Spanish namesake, the equator. The land beneath the eastern jungles now produces oil, but many tribes still live there, especially along the rivers.

Most Ecuadoreans are of mixed Spanish and local descent. There are a few of African descent and some Europeans. Spanish is the official language, although Quechua is commonly spoken, and Roman Catholicism is the predominant religion.

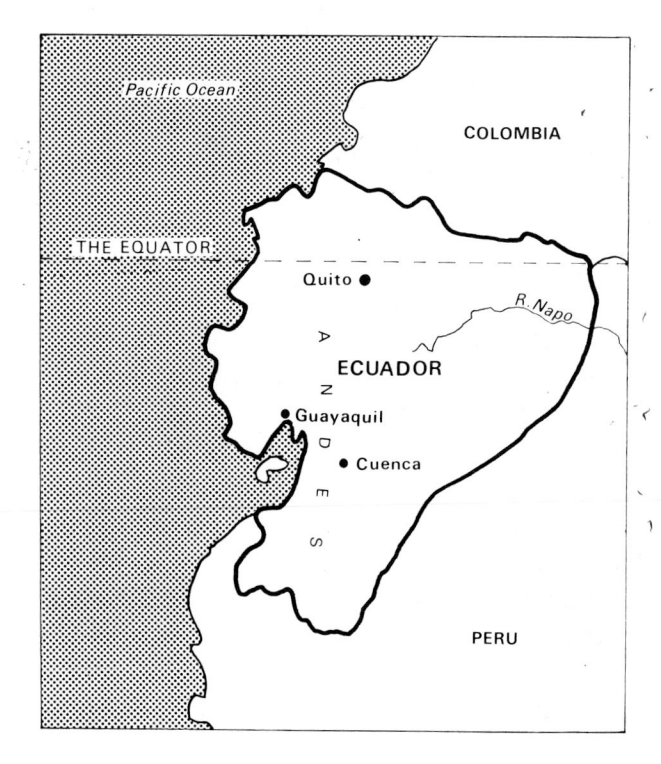

These farming women in Ecuador climb the steep slopes of the Andes to work in their fields. South American Indians have farmed expertly at high altitudes for centuries.

ARGENTINA

Argentina is a big country stretching from the Andes Mountains in the west to the southern Atlantic Ocean. The mountains slope down to great plains. The central plain, called the *pampas*, is rich grassland, a most important part of the country. The south is Patagonia, where pasture is mixed with stony desert. Argentina also owns half the island of Tierra del Fuego. Because it stretches so far from north to south, Argentina's climate is varied.

The early people of Argentina lived in many small tribes with different languages, and most were nomads. They were often attacked by the powerful Inca nation of Peru. North Argentina was part of the Inca empire after AD 1463.

The next invaders came from the Atlantic Ocean. In 1516 Spanish explorers found the big estuary which they called the Rio de la Plata, meaning River of Silver. They thought the river would lead them to silver-bearing mountains, but it did not.

The Spaniards' main center of power and money was Peru. They paid little attention to Argentina at first. They made settlements around the river, including Buenos Aires, which was founded in 1536. Ranchers from Spain began raising cattle on the pampas to feed the people of the river settlements as the population grew into small towns. Any trade went northwest into the Andes, into Spanish Peru.

Warriors of the pampas tribes fought the Spaniards. By 1700 they had learned to manage horses, which the Spaniards had brought to the Americas, becoming even more effective fighters. They charged with lances or *bolas*, a kind of lasso weighted with one or more stones.

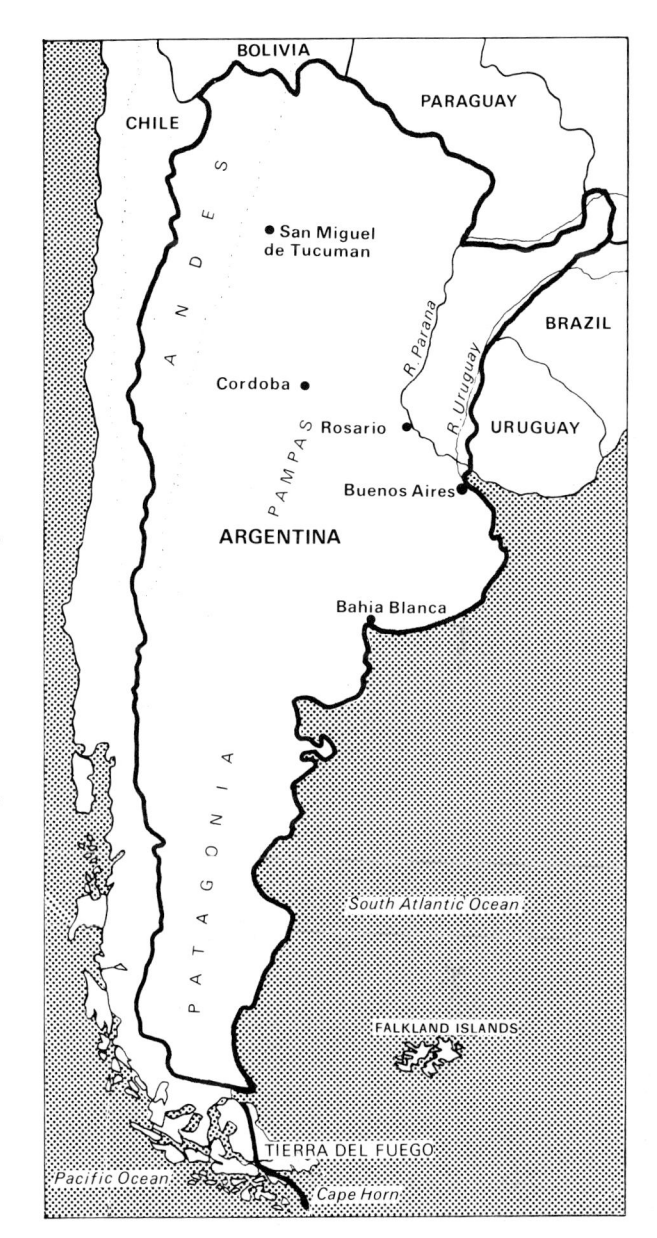

The Spaniards controlled their trade carefully. For a long time all goods had to

Jesuit missionaries were active throughout South America. They built many churches like this one in Argentina.

be taken to Lima in Peru before they could be shipped to Spain. Then in 1780 this rule was changed. Buenos Aires was allowed to export too. The city grew into an important port, shipping hides and other ranch produce. Then the ranchers on the pampas had much bigger markets for their goods. They wanted more land for bigger herds, and fought the natives to take it. The ranchers employed *gauchos* or armed, mounted cowboys. Many gauchos were descended from the pampas warriors, and were skilled riders too.

In 1810 Argentina began a war for freedom from Spain, which it won. But the new country did not give up all Spanish ideas. The enormous ranches were kept. Leaders of the war for independence were rewarded with others just as big. The people native to the pampas were gradually driven out and destroyed.

During the nineteenth century Argentina tried to attract European settlers. Some came as sheep farmers. But most farming was done as big business on huge estates. Ordinary settlers — Scots, Irish, German, Swiss, Italian, Russian, and Spanish — mainly lived in towns, working for the big employers in their factories and railway networks. European companies moved into the cattle industry, and they also began to grow wheat and breed sheep.

With people of so many races and interests, governing was often very complicated. There was frequent civil war.

Most modern Argentinians are of European descent. The language is Spanish. The majority belong to the Roman Catholic Church, but there are also some Protestants and Jews in the country.

THE FALKLAND ISLANDS

The islands are a British colony in the South Atlantic. There are two main islands. The land is bleak and used for sheep farming. The people are of British descent.

British and French settlers were there by 1770, when Spain drove off the British and bought out the French. The British moved back when Spanish power in the Americas had ended. Argentina was one of the independent states which replaced the Spanish empire. It claimed the right to succeed Spain as ruler of the Falklands.

Britain and Argentina have argued over this since 1820. The argument flared into war in 1982 which the British won. (See map on page 55.)

SOUTH GEORGIA AND THE SOUTH SANDWICH ISLANDS

These islands lie north of British Antarctic Territory. South Georgia, about 800 miles (1,280 km) southeast of the Falklands, is a base for scientific surveying. The South Sandwich Islands are scattered over an area further southeast. They have a severe climate, and nobody lives there. The islands are all British dependencies.

CHILE

Chile is a long, narrow country which lies between the Pacific Ocean and the Andes Mountains. A fertile valley runs up the center of the country, and for a long time it was the most important region. Here the early people, moving down from the mountains, were able to farm well. North of them lay the Atacama desert which separated them from the people of Peru.

During the fifteenth century the Inca of Peru conquered an empire. Moving south along the Andes, they had entered Chile by 1463. The Inca could build good roads. They had runners as government messengers. Copiapó in northern Chile was held as an outpost of Inca rule, giving them control of the central valley.

The Inca held northern Chile until 1532. They never controlled the country south of the River Maule. There lived the Araucanians, fishing the long coast and hunting in the thick forest.

In 1532 a Spanish army defeated the Inca ruler, and his empire passed to Spain. The Spaniards had come to South America to spread the Catholic faith, to win new subjects for the Spanish king, and to find gold and silver. They found little in Chile but good land. Like the Inca, the Spaniards used Copiapó as a base. They linked it to Bolivia and Peru by mule trains across the Andes Mountains.

Spanish control did not go south of the Maule either. The river was defended as a frontier against the Araucanians. Captured Araucanians were sent as slaves to the Spanish estates.

Spanish rule lasted until 1818, when independence came after a war which lasted eight years. By that time Chile had a mainly mestizo population, which was descended from Spanish and Chilean native ancestors. Spanish was the main language and Roman Catholic Christianity was the main religion. The central valley was divided into big estates. It was hard for small farmers to find enough land to live on.

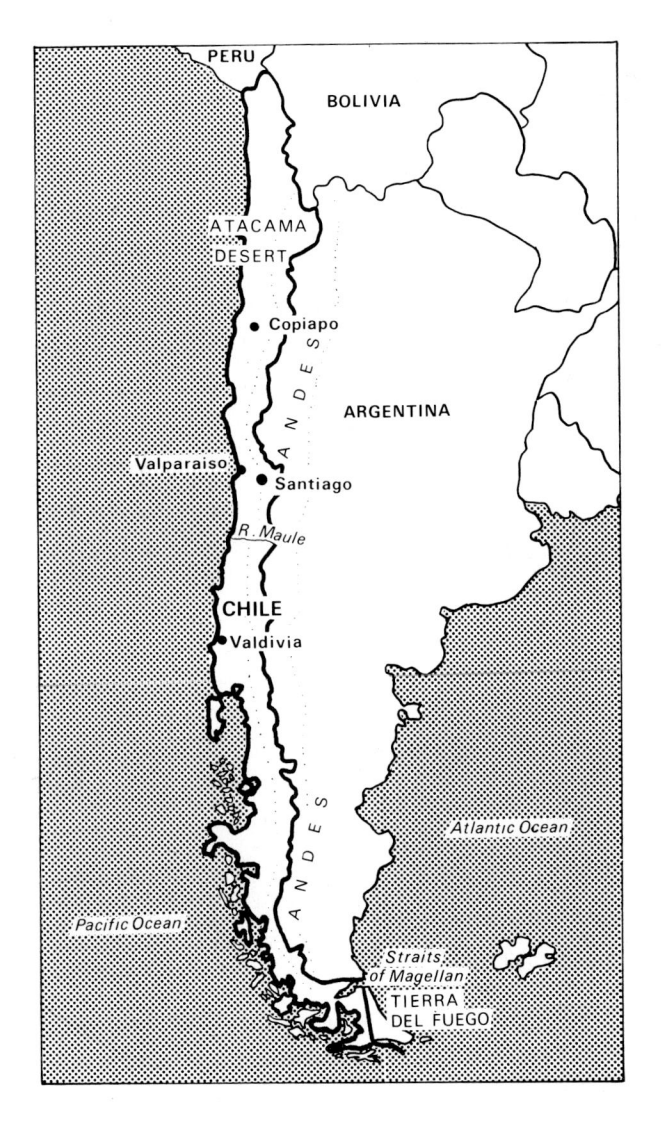

Independent Chile rapidly became a mining country. Silver was found at Copiapó, and then copper. There was a valuable trade in *guano*, or sea-bird droppings, as fertilizer. North Chile grew rich.

South Chile was opened up by German colonists. They went beyond the Maule to clear the forests and the Araucanians were driven farther south. Then Chile sent more settlers to claim the south coast. They went right down to the island to Tierra del Fuego, of which Chile claimed half.

In the north the new industries attracted foreign workers and businessmen. It became clear that there were big supplies of nitrates, a fertilizing chemical, in the Atacama desert. Most of the desert belonged to Bolivia. Chile won it in war in 1883. Industry, and the number of European immigrants, increased.

North Chile grew into an industrial society, with workers who were interested in socialism. The big landowners were still there in the central valley. Trouble between the two groups has often led to revolution and violence.

Today people of European descent live mainly in the cities. Most Chileans are mestizo. The south still has Mapuche, descended from the Araucanians, and Fuegian nomads.

Road building in the high altitudes of Peru is difficult and exhausting. Here, Peruvian women bring a meal for the construction workers.

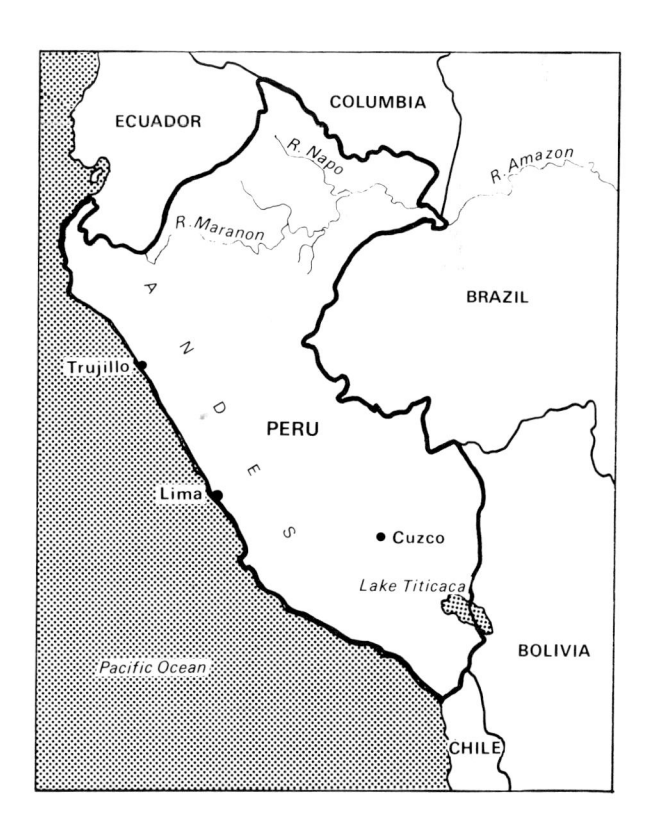

PERU

Peru is a republic on the west coast of South America. Behind the coast lie the Andes Mountains. Beyond the Andes, the forest slopes down towards the Amazon jungle.

The people of the Andes have always been clever farmers. They learned how to take the wild plants of the jungles and forests and cultivate them as crops. They turned wild animals, llama and alpaca, into farm animals giving meat and wool.

Before 500 BC they were already organized into groups, building temples to gods of earth, sky, and water. After 500 BC the coastal valleys were turned into food-growing gardens. The Moche, Nazca, and other coastal people made hillside terraces to save soil from erosion. They took water to their crops by canal.

All this food supported small states, each with a town at the center. Life was easy enough to allow time for art. More temples were built and there was beautiful work in woven cloth, metal, and pottery.

Society was very firmly controlled, so that all necessary work would always be done. Few states had such varied land that could produce every crop they needed. Instead, they sent some of their people to colonize a place higher up the mountain, or with different weather. There they could produce things that wouldn't grow at home.

In about AD 600 these states were conquered by people from Lake Titicaca. The conquerors spoke the Aymara language, and the language spread. They needed to keep their new empire together and so they built long roads linking the different states and cities as centers of government. By about 800 this empire had weakened. People moved away from the cities and the old states revived.

The next powerful state that arose was the kingdom of Chimor in the north. Its capital was Chan Chan, near modern Trujillo. Chimor's king was regarded as a god. His nobles lived in great luxury, and thousands of workers grew food for them. Chimor artisans were skilled with gold and silver. The Chimor were conquered by another tribal nation with a god-king, the Inca.

The Inca were Quechua speakers who came from Cuzco. They conquered Peru between 1438 and 1477, ruling with great efficiency. Their road building was better than any that had been done before. Their officials controlled everything. Like the early states, the Inca made colonies, but not just to farm. Groups of Quechua speakers from Cuzco were settled near rebellious villages to keep an eye on them.

In 1532 Peru was conquered again, this time by the Spaniards. They wanted the country's gold and silver. In 1535 they founded Lima as a port for shipping all this treasure to Spain.

Opposite, the peaceful cloisters of a Roman Catholic convent in Peru.

Below left, the ruins of the fortress of Sacsahuaman stand today as a silent monument to the greatness of the lost Inca civilization.

Below right, three examples of Inca art.

The coastal people suffered from European diseases and forced labor. The elaborate crop farming, needing crowds of skilled workers, failed. The Spaniards replaced these crops with their own crops, which were grown by African slaves.

By 1800 Peru had about 600 thousand original Peruvians left, most of them living in the mountains. There were also many people of mixed descent, Spaniards, and people of African ancestry.

In 1821 there was civil war over the issue of independence from Spain. Peru became an independent republic in 1824. From the 1840s, new industry brought British, Irish, and other foreign merchants. Slavery ended. The planters on the coast brought in Chinese workers to replace them.

Today, most people live near the coast. Spanish, Quechua, and Aymara are the main languages. Spanish Catholicism is mixed with older beliefs in some places.

GLOSSARY

American War of Independence (1775 - 83): A war between Great Britain and its North American colonies, which the colonies won to become the independent republic of the United States.

Arawak: An Indian from one of many tribes native to the West Indies and northern South America.

Aztecs: An American Indian people of Mexico, dominant at the time of the Spanish conquest.

Caribs: An American Indian people of northeastern South America, who were once the dominant group in the Lesser Antilles islands.

Colony: A country or people ruled or settled by a foreign power.

French Revolution: A political movement in France that began in 1789, overthrew the monarchy and the class system, and ended with Napoleon's rise to power in 1799.

Greater Antilles: The large, western Antilles islands — Cuba, Hispaniola, Jamaica, and Puerto Rico.

Incas: A South American Indian people native to Peru. Before the Spanish conquest they were the most powerful group in Peru and ruled an advanced civilization.

Inuit: The people of northern Canada, Alaska, and Greenland, commonly known as Eskimo. They do not like the name Eskimo, given them by a foreign tribe, and prefer to be called Inuit, which is their own name for themselves.

Leeward Islands: A chain of islands in the Lesser Antilles that stretches from the Virgin Islands to Guadeloupe.

Lesser Antilles: The small Antilles islands curving south from Puerto Rico, then west to Venezuela.

Maya: An American Indian tribe of Central America and Mexico. They had achieved an advanced civilization long before the Europeans first came to America.

Mestizos: People of mixed Spanish and American Indian descent.

Missionaries: People whose job is to live in a foreign land and try to convert the people to their own religion. Spanish missionaries were responsible for converting most South and Central Americans to Roman Catholicism.

Mulatto: A person who usually has light brown skin and who has one white parent and one black parent.

Nomads: Races or tribes with no fixed homes who move from place to place, often across borders, according to the food or grazing available.

Privateers: Privately owned ships and their crews commissioned by governments to fight enemy ships.

Roman Catholic Church: A Christian church that accepts the Bishop of Rome, the Pope, as its head.

Savanna: A grassland region with scattered trees, usually in subtropical or tropical climates.

Settlers: People who have come to a country to help develop it and establish a new home for their descendants.

West Indies: All the islands between North and South America in the Caribbean Sea.

Windward Islands: A chain of islands in the Lesser Antilles that stretches from Dominica to Grenada.

INDEX

A
Africa/Africans 10, 11, 13, 16, 18, 19, 20, 21, 23, 25, 28, 29, 31, 32, 33, 34, 35, 36, 37, 38, 39, 40, 45, 46, 47, 49, 50, 51, 53, 54, 61
American Indians 4, 5, 6, 7, 8, 9, 11, 12, 25, 31, 41, 49, 50 (*see also* PEOPLES)
Anguilla (Anguillans) 30
Antigua (Antiguans) 36
Arctic Circle 4, 8, 14
Argentina (Argentinians) 41, 43, 44, 52, 55-56, 57
Aruba (Arubans) 30, 41

B
Bahamas (Bahamians) 27, 29, 30
Barbados (Barbadians) 37
Barbuda (Barbudans) 36
BAYS
  Hudson 4; Samana 35
Belize (Belizeans) 17, 19
Bermuda (Bermudans) 13, 29, 30
Bogotá 45
Bolivia (Bolivians) 41-43
Brazil (Brazilians) 41, 43, 44, 48-50, 52
Britain (British) 4, 5, 7, 13, 19, 21, 22, 23, 26, 27, 28, 29, 30, 32, 33, 34, 35, 36, 37, 38, 39, 47, 51, 57, 61
British Virgin Islands (Virgin Islanders) 32
Buenos Aires 43, 44, 55, 56

C
Caicos (Caicos Islanders) 30
Canada (Canadians) 4-7, 14
Caracas 40, 41
Caribbean Sea 28, 32, 35, 36, 44
Cayman Islands (Cayman Islanders) 28
Central America/Central Americans 18, 19, 20, 21, 22, 24, 25, 26
Chile (Chileans) 48, 57-58
China (Chinese) 13, 39, 41, 47, 51, 61
Civil War (United States) 8, 11
Colombia (Colombians) 26, 41, 44-46, 53, 54
COLONISTS
  British 10, 13, 29, 30, 36, 38, 51, 57; Dutch 47, 51; European 56; French 5, 7, 38; German 58; Portuguese 48; Spanish 37, 61
Confederate States of America 29
Costa Rica (Costa Ricans) 22-23, 24, 25
Cuba (Cubans) 23, 24, 27-28
CULTURES
  African 33; French 33, 38

D
Denmark (Danes) 13, 14, 32
DESERTS
  Atacama 57, 58; Sahara 11
Dominica (Dominicans) 31, 38
Dominican Republic (Dominicans) 34, 35
Dutch Guinea (*see* Suriname)

E
Ecuador (Ecuadoreans) 45, 48, 53-54
El Salvador (Salvadorans) 17, 20-21
EMPIRES
  Incan 42, 53, 60; Spanish 18, 25
England (English) 4, 9, 10
Europe/Europeans 4, 9, 11, 13, 27, 29, 33, 37, 39, 44, 54, 56, 58

F
Falkland Islands (Falkland Islanders) 57
France (French) 4, 5, 7, 11, 12, 13, 29, 31, 32, 33, 34, 35, 38, 39, 46, 47, 57
French Guiana (French Guianans) 46, 47

G
Germany (Germans) 12, 13, 33, 52, 56, 58
Granada 22
Greenland (Greelanders) 14
Grenada (Grenadians) 34
Grenadines (Grenadines) 29-30, 34
Guadeloupe (Guadeloupeans) 31, 38
Guatemala (Guatemalans) 17-18, 19, 20, 24
GULFS
  Campeche 14; Gulf of Mexico 8, 16
Guyana (Guyanese) 47, 51

H
Haiti (Haitians) 29, 32, 33, 34
Hawaii 8
Holland (Dutch) 9, 10, 31, 32, 39, 41, 47, 51
Honduras (Hondurans) 17, 19, 20, 21-22, 29

I
India (Indians) 23, 30, 34, 39, 47, 51
Indians (*see* American Indians)
Indian Wars 5
Ireland (Irish) 12, 13, 36, 56, 61
ISLANDS
  Aleutian 8; Antigua 36; Aruba 30, 41; Bahamas 27, 29, 30; Barbados 37; Barbuda 36; Bonaire 30; British Virgin Islands 32; Caicos 30; Canary Islands 40; Caribbean Islands 37; Cayman Brac Island 28; Cayman Islands 28; Culebra 37; Curaçao 30; Devil's Island 46; Dominica 31, 38; Dominican Republic 34-35; Falkland Islands 57; Galápagos Islands 53; Grand Cayman Island 28; Greater Antilles 37; Grenada 34; Grenadines 29-30, 34; Guadeloupe 31, 38; Hispaniola 32, 34, 35; Isla de Pinos 27; Leeward Islands 30, 31, 36, 38; Les Saints 38; Lesser Antilles 31, 36, 38; Little Cayman Island 28; Martinique 31, 34; Mona 37; Montserrat 36; Netherlands Antilles 30-31; Nevis 38; Puerto Rico 37; Redonda 36; Roatan Island 29; Saba 30; St. Barthélemy 38; St. Christopher's (St. Kitts) 38; St. Croix 32; St. Eustatius 30; St. John 32; St. Kitts-Nevis 38; St. Lucia 35; St. Maarten 31; St. Martin 31, 38; St. Thomas 32; South Georgia 57; South Sandwich Islands 57; Taboga Island 26; Tierra del Fuego 55, 58; Tiger Island 22; Tobago 39; Trinidad 34, 37; Trinidad and Tobago 39; Turks and Caicos Islands 30; United States Virgin Islands 32; Vieques 37; Virgin Islands 32; Windward Islands 35, 38
Italy (Italians) 13, 44, 56

J
Jamaica (Jamaicans) 19, 23, 28, 30
JUNGLES
  Amazon 48; Guyana 39

L
LAKES
  Great Lakes 6, 8; Managua 22; Maracaibo 39, 40; Nicaragua 22; Titicaca 41, 42, 60
LANGUAGES
  Algonquin 9; Aymara 42, 43, 60, 61; Cherokee 8; Chinese 47; Creole 19, 31, 34, 38; Dutch 31, 41, 47; English 7, 13, 19, 23, 28, 30, 31, 32, 34, 35, 36, 37, 38, 39, 41, 47, 51; French 7, 31, 33, 34, 35, 38, 46; Greenlandic 14; Guaraní 43, 52; Hindi 47, 51; Javanese 47; Maya 17, 18, 19; Mixtec 17; Nahuatl 17; Papiamento 31; Portuguese 49, 50; Quechua 41, 43, 53, 54, 60, 61; Spanish 13, 17, 18, 19, 20, 21, 22, 23, 24, 25, 26, 28, 31, 35, 37, 41, 43, 44, 46, 52, 54, 56, 58, 61; Surinamese 47; Tapuya 48; Tupí 48; Urdu 51; Venezuelan 41; Zapotec 17
LEADERS
  Bolívar, Simón 41, 43, 54; Columbus, Christopher 14, 27, 36; Erik the Red 14; Jesuits 52, 53, 56; Sucre, Antonio José de 43

M
Martinique (Martiniquais) 31, 34
Medellín 45, 46
Mexico (Mexicans) 8, 9, 10, 13, 14-19, 20, 22, 27, 45
Miquelon (Miquelon Islanders) 7
Montevideo 43, 44
Montserrat (Monserratians) 36
MOUNTAINS
  Andes 39, 41, 42, 43, 44, 45, 48, 52, 53, 54, 55, 57, 59; Appalachians 8, 11; Guyanas 39; Mayas 19; Pitons 35; Potosí 42; Rockies 4, 5, 9, 10; Sierra Madre 14

N
Netherlands Antilles (Antilleans) 30-31
New Brunswick 5
New Granada (Colombia) 45

Newfoundland 7
Nicaragua (Nicaraguans) 22-23, 24
North America/North Americans 25, 26
Norway (Norwegians) 13, 14
Nova Scotia 5, 11

O
Oaxaca 15, 16
OCEANS
Arctic 4; Atlantic 8, 32, 35, 37; Pacific 8, 44

P
Panama (Panamanians) 24, 25, 26, 44
Panama Canal 25, 26
Paraguay (Paraguayans) 52
PEOPLES
Algonquin 5; Apache 9, 10; Arapaho 10; Araucanians 57, 58; Arawaks 23, 27, 29, 34, 41, 47, 51; Aztecs 16, 17, 20, 22; Basques 40; Blackfoot 9; Caribs 19, 27, 29, 34, 35, 38, 39, 47; Chaco 43; Charrua 43; Cherokee 8, 11; Cheyenne 10; Chibcha 44, 45; Chickasaw 8; Chimor 60; Chocó 44; Choctaw 8; Comanche 9, 10; Creeks 8, 11; Crow 10; Cuña 25, 26; Dakota 9; Eskimos (see Inuit); Fuegians 58; Guaraní 52; Guaymi 25; Hidatsa 8; Huron 5; Incas 42, 53, 55, 57, 60; Inuit 14; Iowa 9; Iroquois 9, 11; Kansa 9; Kiowa 9, 10; Lucayans 29; Mapuche 58; Mayas 17, 18, 19, 21, 22; Mestizos 58; Miskito 21, 22; Mixtecs 15, 16; Moche 59; Mohicans 9; Natchez 8; Navajo 9; Nazca 59; Nicarao 22; Olmecs 14, 15, 16; Pawnee 9; Pueblo 9; Sioux 9; Toltecs 15, 16, 17; Zambos 21; Zapoteks 15,16
Peru (Peruvians) 26, 41, 52, 55, 57, 59-60
Portugal (Portuguese) 43, 48, 49
Puerto Rico (Puerto Ricans) 32, 37

Q
Quebec 4, 5, 7

R
RELIGIONS
Anglicanism 19; Aztec 16; Baha'i 19; Christianity 13, 22, 23, 28, 29, 36, 38; Hinduism 39; Inca 42; Maya 16, 17, 21; Methodism 19; Olmec 14; Protestantism 12, 13, 30, 31, 32, 36, 37; Puritanism 10; Quaker 12; Rastafarianism 23; Roman Catholicism 7, 10, 16, 17, 18, 19, 20, 22, 23, 25, 26, 27, 28, 31, 33, 34, 35, 36, 37, 38, 39, 41, 42, 43, 44; Voodoo 33, 34
REVOLUTIONS
American 29, 30; Argentinian 56; Cuban 28; French 33, 39; Haitian 33; Nicaraguan 23; Salvadoran 21; Venezuelan 41
RIVERS
Amazon 40, 41, 42, 48, 53, 59; Berbice 51; Congo 11; Cuyuni 51; Demerara 51; Essequibo 51; Maule 57; Mississippi 9, 11; Missouri 8, 9; Ohio 9; Orinoco 39, 40; Paraguay 52; Rio de la Plata 43, 52, 55; St. Lawrence 6

S
St. Kitts-Nevis (Kittitians *and* Nevisians) 38
St. Lucia (St. Lucians) 35
St. Pierre (St. Pierre Islanders) 7
St. Vincent (Vincentians) 29-30
Scotland (Scots) 4, 6, 37, 56
SETTLEMENT
through colonization
Puerto Rico 37; St. Kitts-Nevis 38
through conquest
Spain 15
through farming
Antigua and Barbuda 36; Bolivia 43; British Virgin Islands 32; Costa Rica 24; Dominican Republic 34; El Salvador 20; Grenada 34; Haiti 32; Honduras 21; Jamaica 23; Montserrat 36; Panama 25; St. Kitts-Nevis 38; Trinidad 37; Uruguay 44; Venezuela 39
through herding
Mexico 10; Spain 10, 13; Venezuela 41
through hunting
Aleuts 4, 8; Indians 8; Inuit 4, 8
through invasion
Costa Rica 24; Dominican Republic 34; St. Lucia 35
through trade
Britain 9; France 4, 11; Holland 9; Venezuela 40
Slavery and slaves 10, 11, 13, 16, 18, 19, 21, 23, 24, 25, 27, 29, 30, 32, 33, 34, 36, 37, 38, 39, 40, 41, 45, 49, 51

South America/South Americans 21, 25, 26, 39
South Georgia (South Georgians) 57
South Sandwich Islands (South Sandwich Islanders) 57
Spain (Spanish) 9, 10, 15, 16, 17, 18, 19, 20, 21, 22, 23, 24, 25, 26, 27, 28, 29, 31, 32, 34, 35, 36, 39, 40, 41, 42, 43, 44, 45, 56
STRAITS
Bering 4; Florida 27
Suriname (Surinamese) 47
Sweden (Swedes) 13
Switzerland (Swiss) 12
Syria (Syrians) 33

T
Tobago (Tobagonians) 39
Trinidad (Trinidadians) 34, 37, 39
Turks Island (Turks Islanders) 30

U
United States (Americans) 4, 5, 8-13, 17, 22, 25, 26, 28, 33, 35, 37
United States Virgin Islands (Virgin Islanders) 32
Uruguay (Uruguayans) 43-44

V
Venezuela (Venezuelans) 31, 39-41, 45, 54

W
WARS
American Revolution 5, 29, 30; Anglo-French 11, 12; British-Dutch 51; British-French 5; Civil War (United States) 11, 13, 29; Colombian Civil War 45; Falkland Islands 57; Indian 5; Mexican 19; Mexican Revolution 17; Paraguay-Chacó 52; Salvadoran-Honduran 21; Spanish-American War 28, 37
West Indies (West Indians) 14, 25, 27, 29, 32, 35, 37

Picture Acknowledgments — American Studies Resource 9; Barbados Board of Tourism 37; Belize Government Information Service 19; Bodleian Library 12 (upper), 29; Brazilian Embassy, London 48; British Museum 8 (both); Colombian Embassy, London 21, 45; Cuban Embassy, London 28; Ecuadorean Embassy, London 53; Food and Agriculture Organization 18 (J. Littlewood), 42 (P. Johnson), 54 (F. Botts), 59 (C. Sanchez); Le Musee du Nouveau Brunswick 7 (upper); Mexico Ministry of Tourism 16, 17; Peruvian Embassy, London 60 (both); Richard Steel 5 (upper); Sara Steel 14, 15, 22, 26, 35, 40; UNESCO 20, 24, 25, 33, 46, 61; UNICEF photo by Jean Speiser 49; United States Information Service 11 (lower); US Travel and Tourism Administration 13; World Health Organization 23; Young Library 7 (lower), 11 (upper), 12 (lower), 27, 31.